BEHIND ᵀᴴᴱ GREEN VEST

CLAY BONNYMAN EVANS

DailyCamera.com

This book was produced by the Daily Camera.

Published by Pediment Publishing, a division of
The Pediment Group, Inc. www.pediment.com
Printed in Canada

Dedication

To Dave and Dee Hight, for doing things the right way — the McGuckin Way.

Acknowledgements

The author would like to thank the following people for their generous gift of time in providing personal interviews for this book: Dave and Dee Hight, Barry Hight, Jason Hight, Louise Garrels, Steve Wilke, Frank and Joann Hanks, Bruce Ramp, Randy "Doc" Dilkes, Bob Perkins, Bernadette Tillis, Earl Duncan, John Haskovec, Rich Lechman, Rick Case, Igor and Elfriede Gamow, Aron Ralston, Ed Pomponi, Merc Mercure, Tim Ostwald, James Balog, Jeff Milchen, and Denny DiPaula.

Thanks, also, to the many current and former Boulder residents who responded to requests on social media for their favorite McGuckin's memories, stories and experiences.

The staff at the Carnegie Branch Library for Local History, part of the Boulder Public Library system, were extremely helpful to me in tracking down photos, documents and newspaper files about Boulder's early days.

I rue the loss of copy editors and the rise of bad grammar, spelling, punctuation and fact checking in the digital age. Thankfully, I had many excellent copy editors for this book: My wife, Jody, and Daily Camera editor Kevin Kaufman and presentation editor Ronda Haskins. I am grateful for the careful fact checking of Louise Garrels, Steve Wilke, and Barry and Vicki Hight at McGuckin's.

And thank you to Kevin Kaufman, publisher Al Manzi and advertising director Jill Stravolemos, for many years of trust and confidence in my work.

Camera
DailyCamera.com

Table Of Contents

Author's note on quoted material

This book contains a large amount of quoted material from numerous and varied sources. I have presented quotations in the following manner:

Quotes from interviews with living people are simply presented inside quotation marks, with attribution. Example: "You know what makes this place tick?" asks Bruce Ramp.

Material quoted from other media, including books, newspapers, magazines, and online sources, is marked with sequential superscript notes, with sources listed at the end of the book under Notes. In some cases where I have used an extended quote, or several parts of a quote, I have placed a note only at the end, for ease of reading.

Quotes from non-living persons that do not include a note are presented as they were told to me in interviews with living persons.

Keep Calm and McGuckin On

When there is a huge storm, the community's confidence in the store grows.
— Bruce Ramp, employee since 1971

"You know what makes this place tick?" asks Bruce Ramp, looking back on his 44 years with McGuckin Hardware in Boulder, Colorado. "The harsh climate. We can get below zero and above 100; we've gotten windstorms at 140 miles per hour. And when there is a crisis, we've got answers for our customers."

To paraphrase the unofficial motto of the United States Postal Service, in 60 years of business, neither snow, nor rain, nor wind has ever stayed McGuckin's from keeping its doors open and serving not just customers, but the entire community. Everyone talks about the weather, as they say, but *McGuckin's does something about it.* The store has helped pulled Boulder through more than one disaster; it is as much neighbor as business.

"McGuckin Hardware is an institution for Boulder County because they care about their employees and their community. They *are part* of our community," wrote Mimi Elmore, a sustainable landscape designer from Boulder, in the wake of the devastating floods that swept the county in September 2013. "They aren't a chain store. They care about Boulder because it's their home, not just another market."

Family-owned McGuckin's — the store's widely embraced, unofficial name — has weathered its own share of tempests since its founding in 1955, continually defying gloomy (or gleeful) predictions of its demise at the hands of corporate interlopers, shopping malls, big-box mania and online retailing. Ironically, Mother Nature has proved an ally in some of those fights, highlighting McGuckin's community spirit while hurling the worst weather she can conjure at the people living in the shadow of Boulder's iconic rocky sentinels, the Flatirons.

Consider the time owners Dave and Donna Mae "Dee" McGuckin Hight — in 1960 they joined the business started by Bill McGuckin in 1955, taking over after his death in 1966 — were ready to close the store in the face of competition from the national chain Gibson's Discount Center, which opened a store on 28th Street in 1965.

"They were real price cutters. They would buy stuff in large quantities direct from the factories," recalls Dave, 85. "They were 'footballing,' selling top lines below the recommended price, engaging in predatory pricing. They'd come into your store, take down your prices, and practically give their stuff away. They just about put me out of business."

The pressure from Gibson's was so intense that in late 1968, Dave and Dee decided to cut back on hours and close for good if things didn't pick up by spring.

"Our business tanked. We were doing about $200 a weekend. I said, 'Screw it; we're going to close Sundays. If customers aren't going to shop with us then I'm going to spend time with my family,'" Dave says. "I had three young boys, so we started going fishing, sometimes taking off on Saturday night."

Then, on the night of Jan. 7-8, a dry winter wind screamed down off the Continental Divide into Boulder, spinning up the anemometers at the National Center for Atmospheric Research to a record-setting 130 miles per hour.

According to the National Hurricane Center, winds of that speed characterize Category 4 hurricanes and can be expected to cause catastrophic damage: "Well-built framed homes can sustain severe damage with loss of most of the roof structure and/or some exterior walls. Most trees will be snapped or uprooted and power poles downed."[1]

That pretty well describes what happened that howling night, as the gale caused more than $1 million in damage, shearing more than 25 roofs from houses in South Boulder, flipping and pancaking countless trailer homes, launching aircraft at Boulder Municipal Airport only to crunch them back to earth as crumpled balls of aluminum and steel, and heaving power poles from their moorings like an angry Scottish giant. The storm uprooted century-old trees, toppling them onto cars and houses, and killed one emergency worker. The National Oceanic and Atmospheric Administration would later poetically describe the big blow as, "Twister extreme gustiness."[2]

The storm ripped the bright-red roof off the Dairy Queen on Arapahoe Avenue just west of Folsom Street and dropped it right in front of McGuckin's, a couple of blocks away. And, as it turned out, the savage wind also blew out the front windows at Gibson's Discount Center. Which set off the store's fire-sprinkler system. Which destroyed much of the inventory. Which set Boulder's first corporate hardware outlet on the road to bankruptcy and closure.

"I couldn't get Gibson," Dave says with an impish grin, "but God did."

Then there's snow, like the Midwest-style blizzards that smothered the city in December 2006 and January 2007, unceremoniously dumping 45.5 and 27.5 inches, respectively, and turning Boulder into a gray-humped, freezing Duluth of the Rockies. Just a year earlier, the biggest of corporate hardware big dogs, orange-themed, Atlanta-based Home Depot, had finally shouldered its way into Boulder(though an advance guard had opened in Louisville in 2003), opening a huge store at the revamped 29th Street Mall. Arthur M. Coppola, CEO of developer Macerich, had tried to talk Dave into moving McGuckin's into the new center, but he wasn't interested.

"I said, 'You guys leave me alone, I don't have the energy to move again. I'm too old for that,'" he says. "So to spite me, they" — he still refers to them as the "Crossroads Mafia" — "put in Home Depot. I didn't care. We've got a good business."

A lot of people frankly wondered whether a family-owned company like McGuckin's, with its proudly old-school values, could survive a challenge from Big Orange, and for much of 2006, things weren't looking good. The truth is, plenty of shoppers were checking out the new kid on the block, drawn by Home Depot's blitzkrieg advertising and purportedly lower prices, and sales were flattening out at McGuckin's.

But the morning after the first snowstorm walloped the city Dec. 20, people who showed up at Home Depot found the doors locked, the parking lots unplowed and the entire, newfangled mall little more than a sprawling, white-shrouded graveyard.

Over at McGuckin's, the team had slammed into high gear before sunrise, shuttling out in four-wheel-drive vehicles to pick up employees, filling trucks with emergency supplies and inventory from company warehouses east and north of the city, as well as distributors in Denver — everything from small propane heaters and fuel canisters to shovels and mittens. They even made sure there were plenty of sleds on the shelves for anticipated snow-day fun.

"Dave always says you never know when the first snowstorm and the last snowstorm are going to hit, so we always kept 500 shovels in the warehouse," says Frank Hanks, who managed McGuckin's from 1969 to 1992, and from 1995 until his retirement in 2006. "His whole philosophy was that we need to have what the customer needs, when they need it."

"Here we are, serving coffee, picking up our own employees, everyone's happy. The other guys can't even get the store open," says Bruce Ramp, who has worked for the company since 1971.

Scores of red-nosed — and perhaps red-faced —prodigal shoppers practically melted through McGuckin's doors, stomping snow off boots as they entered a warm, brightly lit world of smiling staff pointing them to just about anything they might need. Inside, it was no different than any mild spring morning, with birds singing, flowers blooming and a cheery sun arcing into a pure cornflower sky.

"We got a huge surge from that storm. People went to the other place to find a huge line and locked doors. And we were open. The public said, 'Screw them,'" says Bruce, who credits a late-summer snowstorm — yes, summer; Boulder weather extremes, Exhibit A — that dumped 18 inches on Boulder in September 1971 for kicking off his 44-year career at McGuckin's. "That really reaffirmed that we belong to this community, that this community is our family, and they all came back."

And then there's the rain. *The* rain. *That* rain. The astonishing deluge that drenched semi-arid, high-desert Boulder County — average annual rainfall about 18 inches — with more than 17 inches of rain between Sept. 9 and 16, 2013, including nine inches on a single day.

Just two days earlier, flip-flop- and shorts-wearing football fans had enjoyed the University of Colorado Buffaloes' first home football victory in two years. The day before the storm hit, the city broke a record, with a 93-degree high temperature. Snowpack watchers and meteorologists had been fretting over the mere 14 inches of rain that had fallen from parsimonious skies so far that year, prompting a Daily Camera headline to mildly speculate that clouds predicted to move in Sept. 9 — a "low-pressure system parked over the Utah Basin, fed by a southerly flow of tropical moisture, flanked by a high-pressure ridge to the northeast and upslope conditions" — would give the city a "chance at average annual rainfall total."[3]

By Wednesday morning, much of the county was in full-blown disaster mode, with all roads into the mountains west of Boulder and Lyons washed away, creeks and streams propelling car-sized boulders downstream and roiling across the countryside, flooding many water-treatment systems in parts of the county and leaving residents without potable water. Residents in Lyons, Jamestown and other nearby communities were cut off from all communication and would have to be rescued by helicopter. Basements were swamped from

Erie to Eldorado Springs, from Mapleton Hill to Niwot.

While the county drowned, McGuckin's went into full-blown neighbor mode: "What a storm. Hoping you and yours are safe and sound. The store held up and we'll be open for business today," read one post on the company's Facebook page. "Our Green Vests will be ready to help you recover, clean up, dry out, mop up, or patch up." Doors opened at 7:30 a.m. — "How did your employees get there with all the road closures?" marveled one resident. "Must be strong swimmers!"

"We actually opened early when we saw lines out the door most mornings for a few weeks," says office manager Vicki Hight, Dave and Dee's daughter-in-law. "Customers outside looked so sad and desperate — we had one cashier and a manager and a couple of salespeople to assist, opening some days at 6:30 a.m."

Unlike its corporate competitors, McGuckin's was able to draw from local warehouses inventory to make critical items — shop vacuums, box fans, squeegees, sump pumps, dehumidifiers, sandbags, mold-control products, flea collars, wheelbarrows and just about anything customers wanted— immediately available, while corporate competitors were hamstrung by road closures and other problems. McGuckin's buyers were on the phone immediately with suppliers in neighboring states, and management started sending trucks to Denver and beyond to bring in more desperately needed items, no matter how winding the detours they had to take.

"McGuckin's is the only big store in Boulder County that has a warehouse. We've got trucks coming in every hour," Dave says. "That's a big reason we did so well during the flood."

A big reason, maybe. But just one of many, and not the biggest. As much as anything, the public appreciated the store's familiar commitment to customer service, a keystone of Dave and Dee's business philosophy. Staff handed out bottles of water to customers, linked them to local repair services and kept the public constantly updated about incoming shipments.

"Our neighbors have been calling up all the Home Depots in the state looking for stuff, and I told them that if they just liked McGuckin's on (Facebook), they're updating their stock all the time," wrote Amy McCall of Boulder. "I blew their minds. Thanks, guys, for being part of the community."

"When I put my name on the list for a pump and sandbags I had little hope I would actually get one," Reggie Gray of Boulder posted. "And then I got a call from (the store) not saying they were in, but saying the truck was on its way, and the line was forming, so I better get over there. ... You are a true community resource and not just another business ready to make a profit from an unfortunate event."

"Not only did you always have what was needed in stock (or on the way), your friendly staff was helpful, positive, and reassuring. A friendly voice answered the phone every time I called to ask for advice," wrote CU-Boulder graduate Melissa Cech. "We will be fans for life and consider ourselves successful flood warriors — we couldn't have done it without you."

Employees began to collect tips and "MacGyver" stories — after the famously inventive character on the eponymous television series — spreading the collective knowledge and ingenuity of flood survivors through social media and even a segment on Denver's 9News. With sandbags scarce, "Bags of topsoil or mushroom compost work just as well"; use duct tape and — only in Boulder — yoga mats to create tubes to funnel excess water; use pesticides with boric acid for mold prevention; fashion "gurneys" with broom handles and tarps to haul water.

Newly hired marketing manager Louise Garrels got a crash-course in the long-standing work ethic at McGuckin's: You pitch in, no matter how large or small the job, and there's really no such thing as a "job description."

"Louise was new, and I think she learned a little too much about sump pumps," Bruce says, laughing. "But she jumped right in. There she was, the new gal, right in there unloading the bloody trucks with the rest of us."

During the flood, the McGuckin's marketing team posted a hugely popular logo reading, "Keep Calm and McGuckin On," a phrase that captures the essence of Dave Hight's approach to life. Calm, steady, and confident in his experience and instincts — he can be pugnacious when he wants to be, but it's *his* decision — he grew up learning that it's better to just play the hand life deals you, rather than panic or curse or complain. Mistakes and disasters happen, so don't pretend otherwise. Treat everyone with respect.

"If you did something wrong, he'd just look at you and ask, 'Did you learn from that?'" Frank Hanks says. "He didn't chew you out. He might be a little perturbed, but he never yelled or screamed. He treats everyone like a human being."

Since 1955, through times good and bad, lean and flush, and a drastically changed Boulder, McGuckin Hardware has proved time and again to its loyal customers that it's about much more than making a buck or maximizing quarterly profits: customer service, developing — and keeping — inventory, paying employees enough to support families, paying taxes to support the community and treating everyone with respect. Management consultants, lawyers, corporate competitors, would-be raiders, theory-enamored

management-school grads, cranky naysayers and cynics have all dismissed —
even mocked — Dave and Dee Hight's approach to business. It's old-school,
outdated, inefficient, bound to fail. But come snow, wind, rain, efficiency
experts, Gibson's Discount Center, Sears, the Crossroads Mall, Home Depot or
Amazon.com, the doomsayers have all been wrong.

"Dave is just one of those guys with a heart of gold. ... Dee's the exact same
way," says Frank, who with his wife, Joann, began working at the store in 1968.
"He's really just an old farm boy, and that's how everybody was raised in those
days. You respect your elders, try to help people out, be honest. Those values,
that's what really made the business."

CHAPTER ONE

Forebears

It's the smart alecks like you ... that give young people a bad name these days.
— George Brian McGuckin, aka "Old McGuckin,"
to a daughter's suitor

Hardware, according to the Merriam-Webster Dictionary, is a literal term — "wares (as fittings, cutlery, tools, utensils, or parts of machines) made of metal," reads the first definition, followed by "major items of equipment or their components for a particular purpose."

McGuckin Hardware's roots lie not just in metal, but mettle. Even before crossing the Atlantic, McGuckin and Hight ancestors were builders and craftspeople. After coming to America, both sides of the family first made a living in fields that might be called applied hardware — equipment, construction and farming — and later found success starting and operating successful retail and mercantile-type businesses.

The McGuckins

McGuckin is a name with deep, ancient roots, an Anglicization of the Irish surname Mag Eocháin, which translates as "Son of Eocha" and may refer to a historic warrior chieftain. English spellings of the name have also included McGoohan, McGowan and McGouchin.

Dee Hight, 83, refers to her great-great-grandfather as "the original" McGuckin, but only because he's the oldest branch of the family tree anyone knows much about. His name was James McGuckin, and he was a cooper and barrel-maker born in County Mayo, Ireland. He and his wife, Roseanna, emigrated to Quebec, Canada, sometime before 1835, when their son George Brian McGuckin was born. George — whom Dee calls "Old McGuckin" —

grew up to marry Ella Bunre (born 1840) and the couple began raising a family in Illinois. "At some point," Dee says, "Old McGuckin put his wife and 11 kids on a train to Oklahoma."

Although neither Dee's grandfather, Wilber McGuckin, nor her father, Llewellyn Commodore McGuckin — better known as Bill, founder of McGuckin Hardware —would talk much about the family's past, in 1986 best-selling historical fiction writer Anna Lee Waldo devoted two chapters of her nonfiction dramatization, "Prairie: The Legend of Charles Burton Irwin and the Y6 Ranch," to the McGuckin clan. The chapters focused primarily on famous "Cowboy Charlie" Irwin's wooing of and marriage to Dee's great-aunt Etta Mae McGuckin, but Waldo spends considerable time painting a portrait of Old McGuckin — who went by Brian — as a flinty, sour, religious man with a face "weathered, lined coarse by the action of wind, sun, and rain" and hell-bent on keeping his daughter from marrying a bum like Cowboy Charlie. According to Waldo, Old McGuckin had run a tannery in Rochester, New York, before receiving a message from God telling him to become a farmer, first in Missouri, then near Goodland in western Kansas. It was in Kansas that Charlie was smitten from the moment he saw Etta Mae, a "pixie-like girl" with "eyes like blue violets," at a horse auction. The young cowpoke was excited when he heard his farrier (and folk veterinarian) father had been called out to the McGuckin farm.

"'Pa, those new settlers — the McGuckins — weren't you to do something at their place?'

"'McGuckins? Oh, that was a hound dog with worms. A son-in-law sent word the dog died.'"

Although Charlie's father cautions that, "Irwins and church don't seem to mix well," he can't stop his son from scheming to meet Etta Mae by going to her church and enduring one of "Reverend Dana's sermons on hellfire and damnation." Charlie took a seat just behind the McGuckin clan, crammed into a single pew, where the old man recognized him as an upstart who had, in his view, broken God's law by singing non-Christian music — "Home on the Range"— in public. At an opportune moment Charlie boldly leaned over to whisper into the ear of one of the old man's young sons, Curly, "Tell your sister Etta I'd like to take her home."

But when Charlie introduced himself after the service, Old McGuckin was less than impressed: "'It's the smart alecks like you, you know, that give young people a bad name these days. Singing popular songs. I haven't forgotten. ... I don't allow Etta, nor any of my children, to ride in a whippersnapper's wagon!'"

But in Waldo's telling, Irwin's gentlemanly courting gradually softened the old man's heart, and Charlie was allowed to marry Etta Mae in 1894.[4]

Old McGuckin soon bought a farm in the "Cherokee Strip" of north-central Oklahoma, near Tonkawa, a small town named after a local Indian tribe, members of which still live in the area today. That's where Dee's grandfather, Alfred Wilber McGuckin, born in Stonington, Illinois, on Sept. 27, 1879, married Ina Alice Booth, whose purported history held at least one dark secret.

"My dad always swore me to secrecy, but when I was 13 he told me, 'Dee, don't you ever tell this to anyone, but John Wilkes Booth'" — the assassin of President Abraham Lincoln — "'was a 100th cousin.' Who knows?" Dee says with a shrug and a smile.

Still, while she and Dave were wandering through a Ripley's Believe It or Not museum in Seattle, they were shocked when they came across the alleged — and almost certainly faked or misidentified — mummified remains of the presidential assassin, purportedly discovered somewhere in the desert. "I said, 'Oh my God, that's my dad! It looked just like him.'"

Wilber and Ina had just one child, L.C. "Bill" McGuckin, and, unusually for the time, divorced after just a few years of marriage. Young Bill went off to live with his Booth grandparents on the farm in Tonkawa. His mother married an Oklahoma cowpoke, Ernest Birdsell, and moved to Idaho, where she died in 1920 of diabetes, just 34 years old.

Rough-riding Wilber, meanwhile, headed off to try his hand at the rodeo circuit, riding broncs in big shows from Cheyenne Frontier Days to the famous Stampede in Calgary, where he began looking for work after hanging up his rodeo spurs. There he worked for the Canadian-Pacific railroad, hauling tourists from the train depot in Calgary to guest lodges in the resort town of Banff in the rugged Rocky Mountains some 80 miles to the west. Apparently finding that work a little too domestic, he soon hired on to an enormous Hereford cattle ranch owned by John and Helen Mitchell Wilson near Medicine Hat on the wind-scoured steppes180 miles southeast of Calgary. While working at the ranch, Wilber married the owners' daughter Nellie, with whom he would later have two daughters, Helen and Joyce.

"That ranch was 25 miles across," Dave says, recalling just one of many details he remembers from his many conversations with Bill, who shared more with him than with his daughter. "It took Dee's granddad all day to ride from one side to the other."

When Dee was 13 and living in Fort Lupton, Colorado, Bill surprised her by announcing it was time to meet her grandfather, about whom she knew virtually nothing. Still an only child, she and her father boarded a DC-3 propeller airplane at Denver's old Stapleton Airfield and flew to Great Falls, Montana, then drove almost 200 miles north to Lethbridge, Alberta. From there, they took a taxi about 100 miles east to Medicine Hat — the name is a rough English translation of "saamis," a Blackfoot Indian word for a feathered headdress — where Grandpa Wilber met them in a rickety old pickup to drive them to the ranch.

"We sat three across in the front seat. (Wilber) would drive a ways, then someone would have to get out and open a gate," Dee says. "But for the last part, he said, 'Watch this,' then crossed his arms, put the truck in drive, and steered it into these deep ruts. Well, that took us all the way out to the ranch house."

"He had his own railroad," Dave says.

A small-town girl, Dee had never flown on a plane, milked a cow or branded cattle until that dream-like expedition to the north to meet her cowboy grandfather. "What an adventure," she says. "I just loved it."

The Hights

Dave's family came to America sooner than the McGuckins, when Hans JostHeydt from Bonfeld, Germany, arrived as an indentured servant to English settlers in 1709. The Heydt family tinkered with the German spelling of its name over the years, changing it to various Anglicized versions, including Hite, Hyatt and Hiatt, before eventually settling on Hight.

Industrious builders from the old country, they soon earned their independence, and in 1732, Jost Hite and "16 other German Lutheran and Scots-Irish families from Pennsylvania" came to the area along Opequon Creek in Virginia's Shenandoah Valley, creating one of the state's first permanent, non-English European settlements.[5] That small farming community became an important trading center, and in 1752 it was chartered as the town of Winchester.

"They wound up, so I understand, homesteading and owning a lot of that part of the Shenandoah Valley," Dave says. "They had a lot of ground and a lot of big families, and they were builders, so when somebody would get married, they'd get together and build them a house on 800 acres."

The clan began to spread out across the Midwest, and Dave's forebears almost single-handedly built the now-tiny burg of Walker, Iowa. His grandfather, Jessie LeRoy Hight, was born in 1856 in Walker, and his great-grandfather, John Proctor Hight, served in the Union Army during the Civil

War, along with two of his brothers. Following the war, Jessie Hight and his two veteran brothers bought a wagon and team of horses and drove it to the banks of the Missouri River. There they traded it for a boat, on their way to Yankton, South Dakota, to prospect for gold.

"They didn't find any gold," Dave says drily. "So they all came back and homesteaded in Nebraska."

Jessie Hight married Martha Jane Glass (born in Buchanan, Iowa, in 1858) and the couple farmed 160 acres near Creighton, some 150 miles northwest of Omaha, for three years — the minimum amount of time required to "prove up on" homestead land and gain full ownership. Although several of his brothers also homesteaded in the area, one, Willard Brackston Hight, moved to Presho, South Dakota, where he started the first hardware store in family history.

Jessie later sold his homestead and moved to Norfolk (Dave pronounces the name Nebraska-style: *Norfork*), where Dave's father, also Willard Brackston Hight, was born in 1886. Jessie and Martha also had six other children, Jesse Leo (1880), Joseph (1881), Adolphus (1884), Avon (1888), Meda (1898) and Al (1891).

Just as in Virginia, the Hights made big families, and big houses. Jessie's house towered over the banks of the Elkhorn River, where the Hight children fished and played throughout the summer months, plunging into the roiling water beneath 60-foot waterfalls, snatching up fistfuls of sand to prove that they'd been to the bottom; Willard nearly drowned in a whirlpool one summer and was saved only when his brother Leo dived in after him.

The house itself featured a grand wooden walkway to the road, to give feet a chance to shake off rain, snow or mud before entering. Having apparently inherited the family's carpenter genes, the Hight kids once took advantage of their parents' visit to relatives out of town to pull up the planks and make a clubhouse.

"That didn't go over real well," Dave says.

Jessie Hight worked as a builder but also began learning about the sugar-beet business from local farmers. Armed with the knowledge that beet crops not processed within 90 days begin to lose valuable sugar content, he built the first beet-processing factory in Norfolk, and would go on to build many more plants for the Great Western Sugar Company — started by famed Coloradan Charles C. Boettcher, who would also play a role in Boulder's early hardware history — including in Fort Lupton and Brighton, where Dee and Dave grew up, respectively.

Dave's mother, Lula Ethel Salmon, was born in Bethel, Missouri, in 1887, one of 10 children. She grew up in Norfolk, where William Nelson Salmon, her father, was a foreman on a neighboring ranch and her mother, Ida Alice Daniel Salmon, a housewife.

"My parents eloped to Pierce, Nebraska. My mother climbed out a window," Dave says.

In 1913, Jessie decided to move to the big city and try his hand as a shopkeeper in Denver, where he opened a grocery store on South Pearl Street. But city life didn't appeal to some of Jessie's sons. Dave's father and two brothers jumped at the chance to homestead farms near Quinn, a tiny community overlooking the dry, desolate Badlands of South Dakota. The men would farm during the growing season, then come autumn drift down to Scottsbluff, Nebraska, to work at the Great Western sugar-beet processing plant. Willard and Lula's first three children were born on the farm — Opal Berdeen (1907), Helen Imo (1909) and Willard Ray, known as "Bud" (1910).

A year after proving up on the South Dakota homestead, a good rain year resulted in bountiful crops, and Willard was able to use all that green as an enticement to sell the land and move back to Norfolk, where he built a house and worked a large farm outside nearby Magnet. "Dad turned out to be a pretty good farmer," Dave says, but "bad times hit," and he got into financial trouble. His landlord agreed to move him onto a smaller farm, a quarter-section (160 acres) near Randolph, where he raised alfalfa and clover.

On the farm in Randolph, Willard and Lula had the rest of their children: Doris (1913), followed by a run of six more boys, Warren (1920), Al (1922), James (1923), Jack (1925), Sidney Eugene (1927) and finally, David Keith (1929).

"My brother Warren always said, 'What a time to come into the world, three months after the Crash,'" Dave recalls. "But I couldn't have been born in a better place or time. It was a great place to be, and I didn't know, or care, if we were poor, rich or anything else."

CHAPTER TWO

Growing Up McGuckin

I'll sell you anything I've got except my wife and kids ... and I'll give them away for free!

— L.C. "Bill" McGuckin,
joking to a prospective buyer of his pharmacy

Llewellyn Commodore McGuckin, born Dec. 2, 1907, in Kay County, Oklahoma, never did like his peculiar name — "Commodore was supposedly after a dog," Dee says. For formal purposes he went by L.C. McGuckin, but anyone who knew him just called him Bill.

Though Bill was always tight-lipped about his childhood, he did let on to Dee and Dave that growing up with his Grandma and Grandpa Booth, as the only child of parents who divorced and moved more than a thousand miles away wasn't easy. He was even the butt of jokes among his myriad cousins, the sons and daughters of Brian and Ella McGuckin's 15 offspring. But growing up on the farm in pre-Dust Bowl Oklahoma, Bill learned the value of hard work, and in high school, he took a job with the Brooks and Mulkey Pharmacy in Tonkawa, making $14 a week.

Bill met his future wife, Leo Frances Lacy, at a dance in Tonkawa. Leo, born July 5, 1909, had grown up on a farm in Kansas with three brothers and a sister, Irma. The two girls were responsible for cleaning the house, Dee says, and the only way they could get it done was to lock their brothers outside. But sweeping floors and fending off filthy brothers wasn't Leo's idea of a good life. As soon as she got the chance, she and a friend headed for Oklahoma, where they both got jobs working for the JC Penney department store in Tonkawa.

"She always said J.C. Penney himself would come by the store with a white glove to wipe for dust," Dee recalls.

Bill and Leo married in 1929, and in 1930 decided to move to Denver so he could attend a private pharmacy school. While living at a house on Grant Street, the couple conceived their first child, Donna Mae, who soon got the nickname Dee. After Bill finished his course of study, the young family moved back to Oklahoma. Dee was born Aug. 14, 1932, at a hospital in Blackwell; it would be another 14 years before she had a sibling.

"The (Tonkawa) Indians said Blackwell gets the tornadoes and Tonkawa doesn't, because it's built on a curve in the river" — the Salt Fork of the Arkansas, Dee says.

Always fastidious, having a child inspired Bill toward even greater neatness and organization; he'd even wipe baby Dee down with alcohol any time someone touched her. When Dee was 3 years old, the family moved to Skiatook, north of Tulsa, where Bill worked for a pharmacy. They soon relocated again, to Great Bend, Kansas, northwest of Wichita, where Bill followed up years in sales, service and retail with his first commercial experience with hardware, selling Hughes oilfield drill bits for Farley Machine Works.

Dee has some wild memories of the family's two years in Kansas. One year, as her mother prepared Thanksgiving dinner, someone knocked on the front door, and 5-year-old Dee answered to find a rigger who said her father had been shot in the leg while bringing a little holiday cheer — in the form of booze — to the oil riggers. A rifle fell off a running board, leaving Bill with a lifelong scar.

"I didn't know what was going on," Dee says. "But my mother just about cracked, I think."

Bill and Leo had both loved living in Colorado during his pharmacy school hitch. So in 1938, he found a job at Busy Corner Drug in Fort Lupton, a small town about 30 miles northeast of Denver, named after Lt. Lancaster Lupton, who built a trading post on Apache Creek in what was then part of the Kansas Territory, in 1840.[6] The pharmacy was owned by a man named Elmer Lewis who was, Dee says, "always drunk," skulking in the basement while Bill was upstairs filling prescriptions.

After the Japanese attacks on Pearl Harbor on Dec. 7, 1941, Bill also found opportunities to hone his skills as a carpenter. In 1942, he hired on to build barracks and other buildings for the Rocky Mountain Arsenal, a 20,000-acre U.S. Army site 12 miles northeast of Denver that manufactured chemical weapons — napalm, white phosphorus, mustard and chlorine gas, among others — as well as conventional weapons. The site also eventually housed German prisoners of war.

And though Bill didn't know its precise purpose until after the project was finished, he also helped build barracks and other facilities for the Granada War Relocation Center about 20 miles east of Lamar on the plains of far southeastern Colorado. The camp — more commonly known as Camp Amache, the name of a Cheyenne Indian chief's daughter — was built on a square mile of severe, windblown prairie, enclosed by barbed-wire fencing and guarded by machine-gun towers. The camp opened in August 1942 and at its peak housed more than 7,000 Japanese-Americans interned under wartime policies, mostly from California.[7]

"Daddy didn't know what it was. They all thought it was going to be a camp for soldiers. He was gone all week working down there, and he couldn't wait to come home on weekends," Dee says.

Bill was enormously distressed when he learned the purpose of the camp he'd helped build. After all, he'd been serving chocolate Cokes and conducting business with the numerous Japanese truck farmers living around Fort Lupton and Brighton for years. Even as their fellow Nisei were being rounded up in California, the U.S. government ironically helped these Colorado farmers stay in business, to help raise crops needed to fuel the American war effort.

"His (Nisei) friends came to the front door on Dec. 7, 1941 and said, 'Bill, can we come in? We've been friends, you've traded with us.' Of course he said, 'Yes,'" Dee says.

As the war ground on, the military also began to house German prisoners at camps in nearby Brighton. Dee remembers seeing them milling around outside the barracks when the family drove into Denver.

The United States dropped an atomic bomb on Hiroshima on Aug. 6, 1945, and another on Nagasaki three days later. Emperor Hirohito gave a recorded radio address on Aug. 15, announcing that Japan was surrendering to the Allies, news that overshadowed Dee's 14th birthday (thanks to the International Date Line). Instead of a special dinner at the Pepper Pot, a restaurant famous for its buffalo steaks and stew in nearby Hudson, she spent her birthday at home while her parents celebrated the end of the war.

"I was pretty sad," Dee recalls. "But Daddy said, 'No. This is going to be one wild party.'"

Not long after, Frank Kaufman, who owned Fort Lupton Drug, just across the street from Busy Corner Drug, approached Bill to see if he'd be interested in putting down $400 to buy his pharmacy. When Bill said he only had $500 in the bank, Kaufman said he'd accept $150 as a down payment, leaving $350 in operating capital for the new owner. The two men shook on the deal. Kaufman handed over the keys and asked Bill if he wouldn't mind hanging on to a metal box under the prescription counter until he had a chance to pick it up. Bill now owned his own business and soon enough hired Donna Mae McGuckin as his soda jerk.

Being a pharmacist at the time was an art as much as a science. Bill had to manually pulverize pills with a mortar and pestle, carefully pour penicillin into capsules and mix syrups for customers. The store also sold everything from guns to perfume to newspapers and magazines. Behind the soda counter, Dee not only mixed Cokes and other treats, but kept a Morrow nut display stocked, pouring nuts on a rotating shelf to be warmed by an overhead lamp.

"I loved the smell of the pharmacy and the drugs. It was a little like a hospital," she says.

Bill was able to pay off Frank Kaufman in just one year. He'd sold plenty of penicillin, cough syrup, guns, Coke and hot nuts, but made most of his money on a now-all-but-forgotten game of chance. "Punchboards" were wooden panels with rows of neat holes covered in paper and numbered, each stuffed with a small paper ticket, some of which were worth prize money. Patrons would buy chances and use a small key or stylus to punch a hole to see if he or she had won. This small-bore gambling was immensely popular in the United States from the late 1800s to World War II, with some 50 million punchboards sold in 1939 alone.[8]

There was just one little problem for Bill McGuckin: Punchboards were illegal in Colorado. Every once in awhile the U.S. Department of Treasury would come through the area, going after the slot machines at the Fort Lupton American Legion hall and swinging the net in hopes of nailing drugstores, dime stores and other small-timers for punchboard gambling.

"Marty Sloe over at the dime store used to call my dad and say, 'Bill, they are going to raid you.' We'd grab up all the punchboards, take them downstairs and put them in Kotex boxes," Dee says, grinning. "They weren't going to look in there."

(Remember that metal lockbox Frank Kaufman asked Bill to hold onto? It contained thousands of dollars in illicit punchboard profits, which Kaufman finally came back for a year after selling the business.)

Owning a drugstore wasn't easy for Bill McGuckin. As with any retail business, he had to put up with his share of aggravation, mostly in the form of customers. There was the time one man yanked a rifle off the rack and accidentally pumped a round into the ceiling, which also happened to be the floor of a hotel upstairs. And, strange though it may sound, Bill and young

Dee also had to contend with Gypsies, Basque-Roma families that sometimes drifted through town.

"He started cussing one day, 'Oh, goddamn, lock the doors! Here come the Gypsies.' They didn't have horses, but drove trucks in a caravan, painted black," Dee recalls. "They came in the store, and these little 2-year-old girls wearing beautiful skirts would steal things — soap, perfume, delicate toiletry kind of things, faster than you could watch 'em. But they were beautiful people, so colorful."

Bill was also gradually diversifying, experimenting with other ways of making money besides the pharmacy. He and his teenage daughter spent hours building pens and boxes out of wood, metal and chicken wire for what turned out to be an ill-conceived, three-year experiment in mink farming. Raising animals to provide purportedly exotic fashion for wealthy women proved less than glamorous for all involved.

"Oh, we were always going to make a fortune on mink," Dee says, wrinkling her nose.

Dee and her mother drove over to a hulking, stinking rendering plant each week to pick up rank horse meat to feed the sleek animals, members of the weasel family. The pens and runs stank, and the animals were going crazy in such unnatural environs, constantly running and whirling.

When killing time came, Bill would put on thick leather gloves and haul each animal out by the neck. Leo would then stick them in the armpit with a hypodermic needle full of formaldehyde. On at least one occasion, one reluctant mink sank its sharp incisors into Leo's finger and wouldn't let go until Bill strangled it. Bill and Dee skinned the carcasses, stretched the skins on wooden frames to dry and later scraped any remaining bits of flesh from the pelts.

"Thankfully, the price tanked," Dee says. "I can still smell those skins today."

Bill also bought a bowling alley across the street from the pharmacy, a rustic place where the walls were studded with dusty hunting trophies — deer, elk, antelope. Although he owned the business and the building for several years, he never really liked it, especially having to play janitor and clean the lanes every day.

But to this day, Dee says the most fun she's ever had was the day her dad put one of the deer trophies in the car. Her mother was in the back seat with her baby brother, Ron — full name Ronald Commodore McGuckin, born Jan. 20, 1947 — and she was a bored, mischievous teenager.

"I took the deer head and put it out the window, so it looked like it was watching people on the sidewalk," she says. "One guy was so startled, he said,

'Damn, I thought it was a real deer.'"

It was the kind of prank she would enjoy throughout her life.

Life as a kid in Fort Lupton was simple, but fun. Dee went to the movies, rode her blue Schwinn around town and out to "dirty old" Sand Hill Lake, read Nancy Drew mysteries and "racy" "Lorna Doone," and drove down to Denver once a week with her friend Sybil Horne to take violin lessons in the elegant, three-story Grant Mansion with "Miss Milne." She loved sewing so much that she stitched together elm leaves to make little outfits. In the winter, Bill flooded school tennis courts so the local kids could go ice skating; once they were old enough, they'd go out to a pond on "Mr. King's place, out by the cemetery," build a fire and skate away under the stars. She loved her little dog Flicka, a terrier who followed her home from the movies one day, and hunting for arrowheads out east on the plains with her father. And while never particularly religious — "I refuse to talk about it or argue about it," Dee says — she adored singing with her mother in the Episcopal church choir in Fort Lupton.

She also got a job at Fort Lupton Canning, just down the street from her parents' house, collecting green beans as they slithered down a chute and placing them in cans for hospitals and schools. The job, she says, was "duck soup," except for the fact that she and her friend Patty made just 75 cents an hour to the $1.25 made by the guys on the line.

"My dad said, 'I'll give you $20 a week to come back and work at the drugstore.' But I said, 'No.' I wanted my own job," Dee says.

As it turned out, Bill himself was growing tired of the pharmacy routine. When Dee was 14, Bill Deason, owner of Foss Drug in Golden, walked into the store and asked her bespectacled, balding father if he was interested in selling.

"I'll sell you anything I've got except my wife and kids," Bill joked, "and I'll give them away for free!"

But he made an offer: "You bring me the money, and I'll hand you the keys," he told Deason. The next day, Deason brought a certified check, and as quickly as he'd gotten in, Bill McGuckin was out of the pharmacy business.

He would continue to own the bowling alley for another three years, but now began a new venture with his mother's brother, Charlie Booth, as an "oil-lease hound." The two men knew many, if not most, of the farmers in Weld County, and began negotiating mineral leases with them for oil and gas exploration by Standard Oil of California. No drilling would take place until decades later, with the discovery of the Wattenberg Gas Field in 1970, but working both the oil companies and the farmers, Charlie and Bill made a fair living in a business that involved at least a little sleight of hand, according to Dee and Dave.

"Bill always told me, don't ever kick Ortho (products) out of (McGuckin Hardware)," Dave says, "because Standard Oil" — owner of Ortho — "provided the seed money for the business."

While her father roamed the prairie and cleaned bowling lanes, Dee grew up to wear the blue-and-white uniform of a Fort Lupton High School cheerleader — "Big apple, little apple, Suzie Q! Come on Blue Devils, we're rooting for you!" The girls from Louisville and Lafayette, she recalls, were mean, but the Devils' chief rivals, by far, were the Bulldogs from neighboring Brighton. Still, one of those Bulldogs would catch her eye at a dance when she was just 14.

"I thought he was pretty special," Dee says.

"And I," says the Bulldog in question, Dave Hight, "thought she was about the cutest thing I ever saw."

CHAPTER THREE

Growing Up Hight

Nice girls from Fort Lupton did not *go with boys from Brighton. They had a reputation for wildness.*

— Dee McGuckin Hight on her future husband, Dave

He may have been the baby of the family — "I was an uncle seven times over before I was even born!" — but almost as soon as he could walk, Dave Hight was working on the small farm in Randolph, Nebraska, where his father raised pigs, cows and chickens and farmed corn using a team of horses.

It was a rustic life, to put it mildly.

"We had an outdoor toilet, a two-holer down the hill," he says.

To keep warm in the winter, the family burned corncobs in the stove. Dave was responsible for feeding the chickens and remembers hauling five-gallon pails of water up the hill from a well even at 5 years old. The kids walked to a one-room schoolhouse a mile and a half away, where five of the eight students were Hights.

Then, when Dave was 6, a cousin who had made it big in real estate in Oregon's Willamette Valley asked Willard Hight to come work a farm for him in the northwest. Willard went to town and spent all day dickering with a car dealer, trading in just about everything he owned, including the livestock, and drove home in a new 1936 Chevrolet for the trip west.

One thing he didn't get rid of was a two-cycle, gas-powered Maytag washing machine. He loaded the contraption onto a trailer he'd fashioned out of an old Model T, packed his wife and six youngest kids, all boys, into the new car and headed down the road toward Grand Island, where he hooked a right and drove to Scottsbluff, where a brother ran the Great Western sugar factory.

Relatives tried to talk Willard into staying to work for Great Western, but instead, he took a short detour. Heading southwest along the "Model T highway" to Greeley, then south, he went to visit his father, Jessie, and youngest brother, Algie, who had moved to Brighton in 1918 to help build sugar-beet processing plants. "We'd never seen mountains. We were amazed to see the snow on them yet," Dave says. "I rode up front, standing on the seat. Everything was a thrill along that road."

As it turned out, Brighton was as far west as Willard was bound to go. Once there, Algie talked him into staying, and he bought a 20-acre farm for $2,800, including a chicken shack, barn, water well, machinery and bedbug-ridden house. They still had an outdoor toilet — at least it was a one-holer — though soon enough they got indoor plumbing courtesy of the Works Progress Administration, built for just $5.

It was a time when a farmer could still support a family on just 20 acres. In the heart of vegetable country — Kuner's Pickle Company had merged with Empson Packing Company in 1927, opening canning plants in Greeley, Loveland, Longmont, Fort Lupton and Brighton —Willard planted seven acres of sugar beets, two acres of cucumbers for pickling, two acres of tomatoes and seven acres of alfalfa. When he wasn't working the fields, he found work as a carpenter. Over time, he picked up two more acres to farm as payment for finishing a house for a local landowner and built the family a new house with a concrete foundation and basement on the property, over the years adding a kitchen, living room and bedroom. He later bought two more acres of rich bottom land.

Dave had finished second grade in Nebraska, but was held back and forced to go through it again when he started school in Brighton in the fall of 1936. The elementary school classes were segregated into farm kids, "city" kids like Dave and the children of Mexican farm workers. Separated from his brothers for the first time and self-conscious about being held back, he hated school and "cried half the time," which didn't do much for his social prospects. That led to a fistfight one day on the playground, during which local kids saw that the crybaby new kid was a lot tougher than he seemed.

"I whipped that kid, and all of a sudden I was in with a good crowd," Dave says.

Life at home was hardscrabble, but fun. Dave had a pony — "If you want to teach a kid to cuss," he advises, "buy him a pony." — plenty of friends and lots of room to roam and run. He joined up with a "farm kid gang" that rumbled frequently with the sons of Mexican farmworkers and recalls rushing in to fight for a Jewish boy who had been cornered by another gang in town. He loved to fish and hunt with his father in nearby lakes and the distant foothills.

He could be pugnacious, but Dave was no miscreant. He was a good athlete and an outstanding student, excelling in the 50-yard dash and making straight A's. "I especially loved math and art," he says. Later, at Brighton High School, he played running back for a Bulldog team made up mostly of "big country boys." They played on dirt and took pride in the fact that blood matched well with their red-and-white uniforms.

Though he had been raised to work hard at home, in Brighton Dave also began to show early signs of the hard-working, entrepreneurial spirit that would drive McGuckin Hardware to such heights of success. In sixth grade, he and a friend found a job picking beans for a farmer, Mr. Wolf, earning 2 cents a pound. A couple of years later, he went to work with his brother and a friend for another farmer, Mr. Snell, earning a whopping 10 cents an hour for picking garden crops and weeding. When the old man accused the boys of goofing off and threatened to separate them, they had the bright idea of staging a sit-down strike.

"He canned us, but he still owed me for 18 hours, a buck-eighty," Dave says. "He never did pay up."

It was also in sixth grade that Dave inquired about a paper route with The Denver Post when another boy quit. Unfortunately, he needed a $20 cash bond and a bicycle, "which I had neither," he says. His mother gave him the money for the bond, but it was 1942, and bikes were hard to come by. But a soldier had returned from the war and had to hock his brand-new Schwinn with big balloon tires, which Dave saw in the window of a local store. The owner was asking $50. Dave had $20, but told the proprietor he'd pay him the balance after earning the rest from the paper route, which would pay him $50 a month. He got his first line of credit, the bike, and the job.

His first paper route was the smallest in town, with just 200 customers. Every day Dave folded and tied the papers with twine — rubber bands were in short supply — and delivered them to front porches. Once a month, he billed and collected $1 from every subscriber, keeping a quarter for himself. He soon got another route and was making $75 a month, riding nine miles a day every day, even Christmas and the Fourth of July, for the next two years.

As if that weren't enough, in sixth grade he also took a job at Rice Funeral Home — still operating today as Tabor-Rice Funeral Home — where he cared for the lawn, went on calls with mortician Lyle Rice and sometimes slept at the mortuary at night to take phone calls, all for $35 a month. Dave's days were full, establishing habits he'd follow for the rest of his working life. He was up at 5 a.m. watering, then took off at 9 to deliver the Post. Then he was back at the funeral parlor working from 5 to 8 p.m. When the mortician complained that he wasn't spending enough time on the job, Dave offered to find someone else, since the paper route was more important to him, and he made more money for less time in the saddle.

"I found somebody," Dave recalls. "But a month later (Rice) asked me to come back because the other kid wasn't keeping the lawns watered."

One day during the summer between eighth and ninth grades, Post subscriber Jack Leffingwell, whose father, Archie, had started the Leffingwell Mercantile Company in Brighton in 1916[9], called his paperboy up to the porch. He'd seen how hard the kid worked and wanted to know how he'd feel about coming to work at the merc. Dave thought having one job, inside, at a store, sounded better than his current setup.

"But I've got all these jobs," Dave said. "Could you wait until I find somebody to take the jobs from me?"

In the end, he found another replacement for the funeral home, the Post subscription department hired three kids to replace him, and he took his first retail job at a store that in many ways prefigured McGuckin's, selling just about everything you could imagine — furniture, hardware, farm supplies, window shades — pretty much anything except for food and clothing. Dave worked after school until 6 p.m. weekdays and all day Saturday until 9 p.m.; the store was closed Sundays.

"Everybody was off fighting the war, so it was just me, Mr. Smith and Jim Levister, the old guy who made picture frames," Dave says. "They treated me just like family."

They also treated their customers well and never let a dollar get in the way of doing the right thing, lessons Dave would take to heart.

"I remember one year right after Christmas I was there when a gentleman came in with a little boy, maybe 6 or 7 years old. Jim (Levister) asked the boy what he got for Christmas, and he said he hadn't gotten anything," he recalls. "Jim said, 'Oh, it's my fault Santa didn't leave you anything. He left a trike here for you and I just forgot to get it to you.' He went and got it and gave it to the boy."

As soon as Dave was old enough to drive, he began taking deliveries up to Fort Lupton in the store's 1938 Chevy pickup. Gas was still being rationed in the post-war years, but he was allowed to keep the tank filled and drive it home nights. He was 17 years old when he arrived late at the Fort Lupton grade-school gymnasium for a dance put together by a "flim-flam man" — a little guy with a gold tooth who was trying to talk parents into paying him to give dance lessons to their kids, Dee recalls — and feeling self-conscious because he hadn't cleaned up after work.

"That Saturday night all these guys from Brighton came up. I danced with Ace Dunham, Bob Cole, Wayne Adams," says Dee, who was about to turn 15. "I saw a guy sitting over there in the bleachers, and I asked, 'Who's that?' They said, 'That's Dave Hight. He just came from work at the hardware store and he hasn't cleaned up,' so he wouldn't dance. But the next week he came again, all cleaned up, and we danced to all the good music of that time, songs like 'String of Pearls.'"

Dave, smitten, called Dee not long after, but Bill McGuckin wasn't about to let some Brighton punk date his 15-year-old daughter without blinking an eye. "Nice girls from Fort Lupton did not go with boys from Brighton," Dee says. "They had a reputation for wildness."

But true to the same independent streaks they live by today, Dave and Dee began to see each other anyway. He came by every time he made deliveries in Fort Lupton and her parents were out; he even hitchhiked up some nights when he didn't have the truck. The couple got to know each other while jointly babysitting Dee's baby brother Ron.

"We could tell when the folks drove in the back, and Dave would run out the front door," Dee says.

As it turned out, Bill didn't have to do much detective work to get a read on his future son-in-law and business partner — the McGuckins lived next door to the daughter of Dave's co-worker, Jim Levister, who had only the best things to say about the kid. But Dee didn't know that, and one day she confronted her father, declaring, "I'm going to go with Dave Hight whether you want me to or not."

"That's OK," Bill said. "I checked up on him."

No longer forced to hide, Dave and Dee started spending as much time as they could together. They went to movies — hilarious cartoons with Mickey Mouse, "Gone With the Wind," Roy Rogers Westerns, and Dee especially loved Buck Rogers space-adventure serials. They also took long drives into the country in the '38 Chevy.

"We did a little courtin' in that truck," Dave says, rather vaguely.

"Our kids say we drove in the front and made love in the bed!" Dee says in a half-whisper, refusing to confirm or deny except to say, "We went together all his senior year and kept the road hot between Brighton and Fort Lupton."

Neither one ever had eyes for another person.

CHAPTER FOUR

Prairie, Sea and Mountain

Oh, Dee was hell *on thieves.*
    — Dave Hight on his wife's role at their mountain trading post

Dave Hight graduated from Brighton High School in 1948, and thanks to a teacher who put him on a college-preparatory course, was automatically accepted at the University of Colorado in Boulder. He'd saved $1,000 from his many jobs during high school, enough to pay for tuition — just $44 a quarter at the time — housing, books and living expenses for at least a year.

He didn't have a car, so he hitched to Boulder that first time and rented a room in the basement of Pete's Market at 1818 Arapahoe Ave., just up the street from where McGuckin's would open in 1955, for $15 a month. By the second quarter, he'd found a better deal, taking a private room and board for $17 a month with the McDonough family on the banks of Boulder Creek.

Dave still worked at Leffingwell Mercantile every weekend, hitchhiking back to Brighton on Friday night and "conning somebody into bringing me back on Sunday evening." To make a little extra cash, he'd also collect bottles and bring them to Yockey's Market for two cents apiece.

He continued to excel at school, taking courses in accounting, algebra, business law, swimming and what he calls "dumbbell English." He learned to use the library and particularly remembers one teacher, Ben Grey Lumpkin, an English professor who had written instruction manuals for the U.S. Army.

As hard as he was working, Dave still had time for a little fun. In the winter there was skating at a rink next to Boulder Creek near Yockey's, just below the freshman girls' dormitory. With a new coach, Dallas "Dal" Ward, the CU Buffaloes football team had abandoned the small-time Mountain States Conference and joined the Big Seven. Though pounded by Kansas 40-7 in their first outing on Oct. 2, 1948, Ward earned his first victory with a huge, 19-6 upset over powerhouse Nebraska the next week in Boulder.[10]

"Dal Ward, he was a sporty-looking guy. I saw him for the first time at a pep talk at the old football field," Dave says. "I remember this little cowboy from Wyoming, Woody Shelton, who ran about a hundred yards every time he had the ball."

Dave relished his time at CU, but after just three quarters, he'd spent all his savings and had to thumb it back to Brighton one last time.

"I always gave CU a lot of credit. Freshman year is so important; it's the hardest year," he says. "It was a good school, with good teachers — and in those days, boy, was it reasonable."

Back in Brighton, he started working for Leffingwell's full-time again, which provided enough income for him to buy his first car, a '32 "chop" Ford, which he later sold to buy a '41 Chevrolet Club Coupe. He stayed with the store through 1950, the year Dee graduated from Fort Lupton High School. Dee moved temporarily to Denver to attend the Barnes Business School, but when the Korean War broke out in July, they knew Dave would be called up for service and decided to get married as soon as they could. They married at the Methodist church in Brighton on Sept. 21, 1950, just five weeks after Dee's 18th birthday.

"I've never forgiven my mother, who wouldn't let me make a wedding dress. She didn't think I'd have time," Dee says, furrowing her brow. "So I got married in my graduation baccalaureate suit."

The wedding was small, with just 30 guests, paid for with half of the $500 wedding gift they'd received from Bill McGuckin. Dave's brother Jack was the best man and Jack's wife, Lois, the matron of honor. The newlyweds moved into a small apartment near the McGuckin home in Fort Lupton.

After the wedding, Dave and his friend Bob Cole — who'd danced with Dee that first, fateful night when she first spied her future husband — decided to start a house-painting business. A physician in Brighton soon asked Dee to come to work with him as a receptionist. But that job turned out to be a lot more than answering phones.

"I helped him sew up a 2-year-old kid with a cut on his forehead and tested urine samples by sucking it up from a cup through a bent glass straw and putting it in a centrifuge," Dee says.

When it became clear that the Korean conflict wasn't going to end any time soon, Dave and his friend Fowler Hall decided to join the Navy, to forestall being drafted into the Army infantry.

"It was the difference between getting drafted and enlisting. You just had a lot better opportunities. I did it to further my education, really," Dave says.

The Hight family had a strong military tradition. Dave's brother Willard, whom everyone called Bud, was posthumously awarded the Distinguished Service Cross after he was killed while fighting with the U.S. Army 45th Division at infamous Bloody Ridge in Sicily in July 1943, the day after his 33rd birthday. His brothers Al, Jim and Jack had served in the U.S. Navy, and Gene had been scheduled to go into Japan when the war ended.

"My dad had more boys in World War II than any other family in Adams County," Dave says.

And so, just 21 years old and newly married, Willard Hight's youngest boy drove with his buddy Fowler down to Denver in the autumn of 1950 to enlist in the U.S. Navy. On Jan. 2, 1951, Dave took a train up to the Great Lakes Naval Training Station in Waukegan, Illinois, where he would go through boot camp with some 25,000 other recruits.

To Dave's surprise and delight, he scored so high on basic battery tests for abilities in math, mechanical knowledge, reading, writing and comprehension, that he was one of just six recruits to qualify for the prestigious U.S. Naval Academy in Annapolis, Maryland. But he was soon disappointed when the officers in charge learned he was married and said that fact disqualified him from attending the academy. Still, his aptitude gave him a lot of choices for specialty training. Two of his brothers had served as radiomen, with Jim telling him the story of a friend who got to go radio school in sunny Puerto Rico.

"He said it was like a year's vacation. They even sent his wife down there, and they had a car," Dave says. "That sounded pretty good."

Dave opted for communications, but a tropical vacation wasn't in the works. Instead, he was assigned to radio school in Norfolk, Virginia, home of the U.S. Second Fleet, which had responsibility for patrolling the seas off South America and part of Central America. Having already had some typing instruction in high school, Dave started training as a radio code operator.

"I got up to where I was taking 35 words a minute. We had a slogan: Two dits, three dits, four dits, dash, spells S-H-I-T," he says with a smile.

He and Dee lived in a small apartment in naval housing units next to the railroad tracks and a cement plant. It wasn't fancy, but Dee, for one, appreciated the luxury of having an icebox with plenty of ice. She applied for and got a job in the 5th Naval District stenography pool, typing up financial and budget documents on a long-carriage typewriter for submission to the admiralty.

"You typed it all out, and there was no Wite-Out," she says. "If you screwed up, you had to tear it up and start again."

The couple was an object of curiosity to many East Coasters and Navy personnel, because they hailed from the distant, exotic West. Her boss in the steno pool, Hudie Robinson, was "so dumb he thought we were still fighting the Indians out here," Dee says.

But one day during parade — drills and marching — Dave passed out. He awoke flat on his back and immobilized in the hospital. Doctors told him he had a serious problem with his lower spine and would have to undergo surgery.

"They wanted to operate and, according to them, I'd have to spend a year in a body cast," Dave says. Once he was able, he sought out a second opinion from a private doctor, who cautioned him that such surgeries were not always successful and in fact entailed considerable risk of paralyzing him. Instead, he opted for an honorable discharge for health reasons.

While Dave was waiting for his discharge papers to come through, a neighbor happened to mention that a growing snack-food distribution company, Gordon Foods, needed someone to replace its office manager, who had just been drafted into the Army. Founded in Atlanta, Gordon Foods Inc. (not to be confused with Michigan-based Gordon Food Service) was one of the first companies to plunge into the large-scale potato-chip business, with processing plants scattered around the south, from Tennessee to Kentucky and Virginia. As it grew, the company also began to distribute other snack foods, from peanut-butter sandwiches to "pig rinds" and "nickel cakes"; it would eventually be bought out by Sunshine in 1956.[11]

Dave decided to pay the boss a visit.

"I could tell the head guy wasn't going to hire me because I was only 21. I said, 'Why not let me come in and work a week, don't pay me, and see what you think,'" Dave says, prefiguring the kind of chances prospective McGuckin's employees would be willing to take in the future. Given his past success with similar gambits, it's no surprise that the manager was impressed and hired him not just to look after the office but to sell to the commissaries on Navy ships coming back into port.

Life in Norfolk was often hot — the Hights had no air conditioning to fend off the humid heat of a mid-Atlantic summer — and Spartan, but also decidedly colorful. Towering ships, as big as buildings, from the world's most powerful navies, would anchor along Granby Avenue, and shore-giddy sailors would pour down the gangplanks for some American R&R. It was quite an eye-opener to a 19-year-old, small-town Colorado girl like Donna Mae Hight.

"When the French were in port, boy, you could really tell," says Dee,

recalling the bathing habits of *marinsFrancais* ashore. It wasn't unusual
to see sailors from around the world lying dead drunk in gutters on a
Sunday morning.

There was also the time they went up to New York City with Bill and
Leo McGuckin and baby Ron to participate in John Reed King's nationally
syndicated CBS radio program, "County Fair," sponsored by Borden's dairy.

"We won a bike, some towels and dark-green sheets," Dee recalls, "and they
put our picture in the Norfolk paper."

The manager at Gordon's was so pleased with Dave's work after a few
months that he offered him a position at any one of the company's facilities.
Meanwhile, the couple's life was about to change in a big way: Dee had
gotten pregnant with the couple's first son, Brent, and wanted to move back
to Colorado.

"I asked if he had (an operation) in Denver," Dave says. "I knew that if we
didn't move back to Colorado we'd be going back and forth for the rest of our
lives."

There was no Denver facility, so Dave declined the offer. And in June 1952,
he and Dee packed up their few belongings in his '41 Chevy coupe and headed
back to Colorado, where they would spend the rest of their lives. They rented
a small house in Brighton, near Dave's parents. The most valuable possession
from their time in Virginia was the TV set they'd strapped to an inner tube in
the back seat. Nobody back home had one, so friends and neighbors enjoyed
watching. The men favored boxing matches, but weren't above sitting around
watching the old-school, Indian-head test pattern for entertainment.

Armed with stellar recommendations from both the Navy and Gordon
Foods, Dave started looking for a job through a Denver employment agency.
But he was in no particular hurry, having saved up a little money in Virginia.

He applied at the just-built Rocky Flats nuclear weapons plant west of
Denver. But the prospect of a three-month security clearance process, not to
mention the fact that there was not yet a paved road to the plant — "That car
would have fallen apart!" he says — he turned his eye elsewhere. He had offers
to take over a department store in Casper, Wyoming, and sell milk cartons for
Weyerhaeuser paper in St. Joseph, Missouri, but was set on staying in Colorado
to be near family. Right around the birth of David Brent Hight on Dec. 5, 1952,
Dave took a job as an auditor and "troubleshooter" for Carlson & Frink Dairy,
founded south of Denver in 1896 as the Larkspur Creamery. Dave traveled
to seven remote farms and "cream stations," from Castle Rock to Kiowa,
Steamboat Springs to Sterling. Although there were plenty of other dairies

— Alba in Boulder, Nevada Creamery in Colorado Springs, Clover Leaf in Greeley, and others — Carlson & Fink was the largest independent in the state.

"If a branch was having trouble, I'd put five shirts and five pairs of shorts in a bag, hop in a company car and take off for Sterling or wherever to straighten things out" and clean up the books, Dave says.

Dave and Dee continued to live in Brighton, where he bought and fixed up a little house that had once been a chicken shack. Their second son, Barry Lynn, was born in 1955, and Robb Allen, the youngest, in 1956, in Brighton. They sold the house in 1957 and bought a house at 1810 South Kearney St. in Denver, to reduce Dave's commuting time.

But in a harbinger of America's economic future, consolidation fever was beginning to hit the dairy business, and chains were on the rise. John Garrett, the controller of Carlson & Fink, had bought Royal Crest, and in 1958, Ohio-based Borden — the 800-pound gorilla of dairy companies, home of Elsie, America's favorite cartoon "spokescow" — moved in.

"The marketplace was really changing. We had mostly served all the mom-and-pop grocery stores, but the chains by then were pretty well taking over," Dave says. "I saw them put all the honest people out of business."

Although he agreed to stay on with Borden as an accountant, he left the company six months later when he was told he would be transferred to Texas as part of a "consolidation." The end of Dave's career in the dairy business provided a stark lesson in how not to run a business, and it would profoundly shape and influence the values that he would later instill at McGuckin Hardware. But his long apprenticeship was still not over.

Dave had heard from Don Oakes, proprietor of I.K.O. (Isbell-Kent-Oakes) Dry Goods in Denver that George Coulter was looking for someone to operate his legendary Fremont Trading Post, which served some 300 miners working at the famous Climax Molybdenum Mine just outside Leadville. In 1933, Coulter had leased seven acres from the mine on 11,319-foot Fremont Pass with help from his brother Bill, who worked for the mine and would become president of Climax Molybdenum in 1935. Although technically a private venture, the post served as a company store, selling "everything a Climax miner would need for the job," including hard hats, gloves, overalls, rubber-soled boots, carbide lamps, tool belts, and food, not to mention a bar, dubbed the Slop Chute by miners who came to drink, play cards and try their luck on slot machines.[12]

"Any man with a Climax payroll number didn't need cash. ... George issued his own company currency — paper chits in dollar denominations and 'Good in Trade at the Fremont Trading Post,' available in books of $5.00, $10.00 and

$20.00," writes Stephen M. Voynick in "Climax: The History of Colorado's Climax Molybdenum Mine."[13]

Prices were steep, especially during winter months when the pass was snowed in, leading to jokes about George's "high altitude tax," but there was simply nowhere else to shop. Trading-post purchases were deducted from paychecks, which offered employees the opportunity to begin building good credit, but many couldn't pull it off, ending up, as Merle Travis' famous mining lament "Sixteen Tons" puts it, owing their souls to the company store.[14]

Dave Hight had always been a flatlander, the kid who could barely fathom the mountains he first saw while standing in the front seat of a Chevy sedan at age 7, but this opportunity sounded like too big an adventure to pass up. He contacted George Coulter, got the job, sold the house in Denver and moved his young family a mile closer to heaven in September 1959 to run a good, old-fashioned trading post.

Life at Climax was like nothing Dave, Dee or their three boys had ever experienced, or ever would again. The winter of 1959-60, it snowed 37 feet on Fremont Pass. The boys got their first taste of skiing when Climax native son Dave Gorsuch, future co-founder of Vail Resorts, helped Brent put up a rope tow that they could see right out their back window. Basque sheepherders would visit the store once the herds got into the high country in June, and instead of filling up a car, carry-out boys loaded enough supplies to last through the summer into packs hauled by donkeys. Robb often toddled into the bar and dangled his 3-year-old legs off a stool, hoping someone would buy him a Coke.

Remembering his days with Leffingwell Mercantile, and honing one aspect of McGuckin's formula for success, Dave did whatever needed doing to keep the store running and his family in beans, whether carrying out supplies for miners, checking inventory or working the floor.

"They just thought I was a janitor up at Climax," he says.

Dee not only helped with the accounts but also became the de facto family muscle, patrolling the aisles in search of shoplifters.

"Oh, Dee was *hell* on thieves," Dave says, sounding proud.

That pretty well sums up McGuckin's approach to the inevitable, if infinitesimal, number of customers who try to leave the store without paying. The store has always refused to coddle alleged offenders, calling police in every case. But the policy isn't intended to be punitive so much as be a lesson in consequences that may inspire someone to reconsider his or her choices. (Sometimes that could take awhile. Dee recalls one man who came in and wanted to pay the store back for shoplifting a quarter-century earlier.)

"Whenever someone got in trouble, Dave always wanted to know, 'Did you learn something?'" Frank Hanks says.

But once again, the rising tide of corporate buyouts and mergers would intrude on the simple, honest, entrepreneurial world Dave and Dee had learned as kids and continued to embrace as they entered the working world. Just five months after the Hights took over the Fremont Trading Post, Denver-based mining giant American Metal Company — started in 1887 by a consortium of German bankers, New York traders and Rocky Mountain miners, though shorn of German ownership at the outset of World War II — completed a merger to create American Metal Climax, or AMAX. The new company wanted to "modernize," and that meant doing away with the independent Climax community, the trading post and most definitely old-school practices like deducting purchases from paychecks. Company managers had already decided in summer 1959 that "The Climax community had outlived its usefulness and was standing squarely in the way of future mine and mill development."[15]

Eyeing AMAX's practices elsewhere, a Leadville weekly paper warned that "The corporation will invest in housing, new media, etc. They pay the workmen and then the workmen pay them in return, for housing, and in some cases for the very food they eat. … The next move is usually to start taking over the shops, to start loan companies and banks, and to gain complete control over the populace."[16]

In February 1960, company managers shocked employees and residents when they announced that AMAX had already sold nearly every building in the community, including the school, hospital and most housing, to an Ohio real-estate developer. All miners would be moved to nearby Leadville, where they could buy homes financed by the developer.[17] And that was the end of the trading company.

"They just sold off the town," Dave recalls, shaking his head. "They bought the store, and I only stayed up there to close out the books."

He and Dee had no idea what they would do next. Fortunately for them, during the time they had been working so hard to support their young family, bouncing around from the dairy business to the trading post, from the plains of Denver to the snowbound heights of Fremont Pass, Bill McGuckin had made a few life changes himself, and he extended them a helping hand.

CHAPTER FIVE

Back to Boulder

I suggested he include hardware items.
— Dave Hight's advice to his father-in-law, Bill McGuckin

Tired of cleaning, Bill McGuckin closed down his bowling alley after just three years, and by 1950 was making his living mostly as an oil-lease agent with his uncle Charlie Booth. His daughter was all grown up, married and soon to be a mother, and though his son Ron was still a toddler, Bill decided it was time to shake things up.

An avid hunter and fisher, Bill had often plied the waters of the humble "lakes" — Americans from wetter climes scoff that Colorado has anything more than ponds — in Adams and Weld counties in the fiberglass boat he'd made himself, the Ron Dee. But he was also willing to travel to mountain trout streams and plentiful foothill deer herds in the fall, and that meant a straight shot west from Fort Lupton along what's now Colorado Highway 7 — better known as Arapahoe Road — into Boulder County, where the Rocky Mountains didn't merely rise, but punched almost vertically out of rolling grassy plains into towering sentinels of ancient sedimentary rock.

"He always loved Boulder," Dee says of her father, so in 1953 he rolled up his old life and headed west.

Having spent the first part of his professional life working for other people, then owning businesses that supported his family but didn't ignite any real passion and taking on the semi-itinerant, not-quite-conventional role of a slick negotiator between landowners and big oil, Bill planned to do something he truly loved when he came to Boulder. It was obvious: He would open a sporting-goods store and spend his days communing with — and selling to — his fellow outdoorsmen.

But when he explained his plans to his son-in-law, Dave had his doubts.

"I told him he was going to have a hard time making a living out of just sporting goods at that time," Dave says. "I suggested he include hardware items."

Dave was prepared to offer his father-in-law a wealth of advice, experience and, perhaps most importantly, personal connections with the best wholesalers and distributors — known to retailers of the time as "jobbers," all were family-owned and ran their businesses the old-fashioned way Dave liked — within a thousand miles of Boulder.

"I had all that good experience working at Leffingwell Mercantile. As an accountant there I realized there were four steps to distribution: the factories, the factory reps, the salesmen out on the road, and the jobbers," Dave says.

He'd worked with reps of such trusted names as Scott's fertilizers, Stanley tools, Disston saws out of Philadelphia, True Temper hardware, Jacobsen lawn mowers and countless others, and all the best family-owned jobbers, including Townley Metal and Hardware out of Kansas City, Nebraska-based Dutton Lainson, Holmes Hardware of Pueblo, and Whitney Sporting Goods in Denver. One of the earliest lessons Dave learned in business was to cultivate personal relationships with his distributors and salespeople, one of the defining characteristics at McGuckin Hardware for six decades, and he told Bill he'd be glad to make all the introductions he might need.

"The jobbers would run a warehouse, and they'd have a salesman call on you once a week. They'd hand-write your order for the warehouse, and then send out trucks to all the little stores," Dave says.

Many modern Americans have been taught to disdain the very concept of a "middleman," but the factory-distributor-retail model used to be what made small business run in America. "A good jobber was worth more than what it cost you," Dave says. "In turn, you were supporting a lot of other dealers, and factories had automatic markets to sell to. You were helping to employ people you didn't even know."

Even so, Bill had picked a tough place to compete in Boulder, where the undisputed champion in the hardware game, Valentine Hardware, could thump its chest while standing atop a storied history with roots in the city's earliest days. By comparison, McGuckin was a 98-pound weakling.

Hardware was literally the foundation of the city that would grow up to become Boulder, Colorado. On the eve of the mad rush for Rocky Mountain gold in the late 1850s, rumors began to circulate among pioneers in the Kansas and Nebraska territories that the hills and mountains west of Denver were gleaming with riches.

A band of Southern Arapaho Indians, led by Chief Niwot (which means "left hand" in the Arapaho language) spent warmer months hunting buffalo on the eastern plains and wintered along the banks of what would later be dubbed Boulder Creek. Skilled traders, the Arapaho maintained alliances with the more nomadic Cheyenne Indians, led by Black Kettle. As the first of some 150,000 prospectors invaded the western Kansas Territory in search of gold, and 35,000 set up permanent camps along the Colorado foothills, Niwot learned the English language and initiated trading and commerce with the newcomers.[18]

In November 1858, a group of Nebraska Territory squatters led by Capt. Thomas Aikens arrived in a broad, alluvial valley and built a camp near the mouth of Boulder Canyon. Not long after, 61 white men wrote and signed the Article of Organization creating the Boulder City Town Company on Feb. 10, 1859.[19]

"Within Boulder's first years, most men attempted mining, while others knew that profits would come from supplying the miners," writes Mona Lambrecht of the Boulder History Museum. "Despite being called a 'hideous collection of frame houses on a burning plain' by Isabella Bird in 1873, Boulder's businesses grew."[20]

By 1860 there were more than 850 white settlers, including many women and children, living in the area, and businesses had sprung up all along what was already called Pearl Street. The only avenue in the new settlement not to feature an arboreal name, the origins of the muddy main drag's name remain a mystery. Some claim the eponymous Pearl was a madam who ran a brothel, but the more likely theory seems to be that it was named after the wife of one of the men who signed the town's founding document. Whatever the name's provenance, it swiftly became the key commercial area in Boulder. Blacksmiths, tool-mongers and purveyors of tough mining garments were all progenitors of Boulder's hardware business. It's not entirely certain who opened the first true hardware or mercantile store, but Frederick A. Squires and Jonathan A. Tourtellot, two friends who married twin sisters in New York state and came to Boulder in 1860, may deserve that claim to fame.[21]

There was a saloon but no store in Boulder when Squires and Tourtellot bought one of the town's 60 log cabins, a simple structure built by William A. Davidson and Samuel M. Breath on the northeast corner of 11th and Pearl streets. They built the two-story "Boulder House" on the opposite corner and opened a boarding business and kitchen, taking IOUs from miners on the side to sell them some hard goods.[22] By the end of the 1860s, there were 77 buildings and numerous businesses in town, including flourmills, sawmills, brickyards, blacksmith shops and general stores.[23]

But the first business that probably deserves the hardware or mercantile label might well have been the store Squires and Tourtellot opened at 12th and Pearl in the city's first brick building, constructed by city father Andrew Macky, whose name still graces the soaring Macky Auditorium on the CU-Boulder campus today. An advertisement for their store in the Feb. 17, 1869, issue of the Boulder Pioneer hawked just about anything you can think of, including "Dry Goods; Groceries; Clothing; Boots and Shoes; Hats and Caps; Hardware; Tinware; Queensware" — a brand of fine china — "Glass and Putty ... Mining Tools ... Agricultural Implements ... Garden Seeds."[24] Other brick-and-mortar hardware stores began to crop up after that, including Welch and Co., which was housed in a two-story brick structure at 14th and Pearl, built by A.L. Welch in 1875 after he razed the settlement's first wood-frame home, built in 1860 by Macky.[25] I.T. McAllister owned a hardware business on Pearl Street in 1878 that stayed in business until 1932.

But by far the most prominent of Boulder's early hardware barons was Charles Boettcher, who left his native Germany at age 17 and arrived in the new Colorado Territory in 1872. Boettcher, who would go on to become one of the state's wealthiest and most famous early citizens, had already opened stores in Cheyenne, Greeley and Fort Collins when he came to Boulder in 1876, the year Colorado became the 38th state admitted to the union. Two years later, he built the soaring Boettcher Building at 1144 Pearl Street, so enormous that it was simply called the Boettcher Block. Upstairs, he opened Boettcher Hall for concerts and public and private social events. Downstairs, he started the first of a long series of hardware businesses that would operate out of the building until 1973, providing a home for McGuckin's main competition.

"The Boettcher Block was Boulder's main center for hardware, stoves, and commercial vehicles," writes Boulder historian J.B. Schoolland. "At times the sidewalks were so cluttered with various merchandise that it was almost impossible to pass."[26]

But Boettcher lost interest just a year later and sold out to his brother Herman, who owned a hardware store in Cheyenne. Charles was off to find even greater fortune, first in Leadville, where he manufactured the blasting powder to open up mining tunnels, and started an electric company and the Ideal Cement Company. He later moved to Denver, where he continued to build his fortune in real estate, ranching and beet farming, eventually starting Great Western, the sugar giant for whom early McGuckins and Hights had built processing plants and silos.

Herman Boettcher sold the Boulder store to Isaac Berlin several years later, and Thomas F. Feeney bought it in 1882, converting the concert hall upstairs to a ballroom and dance hall. Feeney subsequently sold the building and hardware store to F.C. Moys, who ran it until 1906.[27] By then, the city had a population of some 8,000, and hardware businesses had sprouted up all over the place. A 1904 business directory lists no fewer than nine: D.H. Dickson, 1643 Pearl; Isaac T. Earl, 1825-27 Pearl; Hub, 2014 12th; F.C. Moys in the Boettcher Building; Noah's Ark, 1445 Pearl; Rutter Hardware and Grocery, 15th and Pearl; M.S. Whiteley, 1413 Pearl; as well as G.N. Fairman and F.E. Wilson (who also co-owned a hardware store in Eldora), 1113 Pearl; and Drake-Petsch on — what else? — Pearl Street.[28]

All those Pearl Street addresses demonstrate one hard-and-fast maxim of Boulder's early commercial history: Location, location, location, and if you wanted to sell hardware — or anything else — you needed to be on Pearl Street, or certainly no more than a block or two away. Such thinking would hold sway for decades, but following World War II, especially, upstart businesses would begin to sprout up further afield, including Bill McGuckin's place on Arapahoe.

But of those nine Boulder hardware businesses, only one would really matter beyond the first couple of decades of the 20th century — whichever occupied the historic Boettcher Building, no matter the owner. In 1905, that was Frank E. Wilson, who had bought the store from Moys and would later hire a manager from Iowa named John W. Valentine.

Born in 1875, John Valentine had grown up in Casey, Iowa (three hours east of Walker, the town built by Dave Hight's German ancestors). He worked for his father as a teenager and after graduation from high school, and he later bought and operated his own store in nearby Fontanelle, Iowa, for two years before deciding to relocate to Boulder.

Valentine went to work as a clerk for Wilson on March 1, 1905, earning $65 a month. Within six months, he had all but taken over the store from Wilson, who often suffered respiratory problems.[29]

"It will pay you to better acquaint yourself with our goods and our prices," reads a loquacious, sober — and to modern ears, drily comical — advertisement in the Sept. 2, 1905, Daily Camera. "We are, and always have been, determined to give satisfaction and to make our store a pleasant and profitable trading place for you. If you will study our prices and methods, you too, like so many of your neighbors, will let us have your patronage. Your best interests demand it.

"The Wilson Hardware Co.

"J.W. Valentine, Manager."

In 1907, Valentine and his partner, Harry Fields, bought shares of the business from Wilson. Following a nationwide financial panic in October 1907, known as the Knickerbocker Crisis, Wilson "lost his health" and was ordered by his doctor to move to a climate where he would find it easier to breathe. Valentine bought out Wilson's and Fields' shares in 1908 and bought the Boettcher Building itself in 1920.[30] However, he continued to run the business as Wilson Hardware until the corporation papers expired in 1926, when he renamed it Valentine Hardware.

In those early days, Valentine himself hitched up horses to a buggy and traveled from mining camp to mining camp drumming up business, "Through his progressiveness and visits the Valentine store soon won the bulk of trade of mine operators, contractors and farmers."[31] Along with grocer Ralph Joyce, he extended credit for staples to Emma Birge, aka Emma (or Em) Bugtown, one of the more prominent denizens of "Bugtown" — because of the bedbugs — or "The Jungle," the red-light district on the flats along Boulder Creek between 9th and 6th streets.[32] Variously described as "an early unfortunate character in Boulder"[33] and "one of the most peculiar characters in the history of Boulder,"[34] the "Queen of the Jungle" ran a brothel and was accused of committing various crimes and misdemeanors during her reign. Neither Valentine nor Joyce ever required Her Highness to pay for thousands of dollars in purchases.[35]

But besides being charitable to EmBugtown, John Valentine also built Boulder's first hardware behemoth.

"The whole thing started as the dream of two young fellows back in 1905," Valentine told a Daily Camera reporter on the 25th anniversary of the first, unofficial partnership with Wilson in 1906. "The gray mule of yesterday has been replaced by the gas delivery wagon of today."[36]

Valentine more than doubled the capacity of the store over the years, and his stature increased steadily in Boulder. He served as president and chairman of the board of the Mercantile Bank and Trust, was an early member of Rotary, serving as president in 1924-25, and was a founding member of the original Boulder Country Club on Arapahoe Road. He was named Hardware Man of the Year by the National Retail Hardware Association in 1955, and the business was named Brand Name Retailer of the Year in 1951 by the Brand Names Foundation. He also engaged in a long-running, friendly debate on the pages of the Daily Camera with the publisher, "Colonel" Lucius C. Paddock, answering editorials with rebuttals in paid advertisements.[37]

By 1955, Valentine Hardware was Goliath. But that year, a David named

Bill decided to open his own little hardware store, far from the prime downtown business district.

Bill McGuckin's venture commenced Friday, Sept. 9, 1955 —a classic late-summer day in Boulder, with clear skies and an afternoon high of 90 degrees — when he unlocked the doors of a 3,500-foot space at 2645 Arapahoe Ave. (present site of Changes in Latitude travel store) in Boulder's first shopping center, Arapahoe Village, owned by the Platt family, which operated Western Cutlery. By a quirk of geography, the property was actually located on county property; so technically, the first shopping center to be built within city limits was Basemar, which opened the same year. Arapahoe Village South was built at the same time by the Murchison family of Texas on a former golf course, bounded by Folsom, Arapahoe and 28th streets. Arapahoe Village North would soon follow, extending the development to Canyon Boulevard.[38]

The four employees at McGuckin Hardware & Sporting Goods, including Bill, greeted customers wearing green vests, the forebears of today's staff attire.

"That was to honor the Irish," Dave says.

"'Bill' invites you to come in and see his full line of Hardware-Sporting Goods-Grass Seed" announced a two-color — red and black ink on white — advertisement in the Daily Camera, the first of literally thousands to follow. The ad invited customers to register for free prizes — "No One Leaves Without a Gift!" — including an electric Sunbeam frying pan, a $25 (nearly $220 in 2015 dollars) Wright-McGill fishing kit, a General Electric hand mixer and Melmac dinnerware. The drawing would be held at 8 p.m., closing time, Saturday the 10th, and customers had to be present to win.

McGuckin's neighbors in the Arapahoe Village shopping center also advertised on the spread, including Anderson Drug, Clair's Super Market, Haskins Pastry Shop, BauldieMoschetti's Boulder Liquor, Dugout Cleaners and the Phillips-Cline real-estate agency. There were well wishes from contractor Frank C. Myers, Rayback Plumbing, Boulder Metal Products, Bo-Col Welding Works, Boulder Sand & Gravel Co. and other hardware-connected businesses.

Perhaps most memorable, just east of McGuckin's, was Pete Taylor's semi-legendary Lamp Post Restaurant and Bar (1958-74), one of only a few establishments inside Boulder's "dry" city limits where people could drink alcohol in a public establishment, thanks to the fact that it stood on an island of county property.

"Being one of the few places you could drink close to campus gave us a very secure operation, but once Boulder went 'wet' (in 1967) that blessing was gone," says Robert Trembly, who came to Boulder in 1962 to attend CU and worked as a waiter, bartender and manager at the Lamp Post. He recalls countless visits by "Mr. McGuckin (Bill) … then Dave … then Frankie (Hanks) and the fellows. … I always felt I got the very best education as I got the practical material during the day … and then the reality from the same professors in the evenings over a brew."

Dave frequented the restaurant often, using it as a place to hold casual meetings with employees, salesmen and distributors, even as a recruitment station of sorts.

"I waited on Dave, and he always told me, 'If you ever leave this place, come see me,'" says Frank Hanks, who was a dishwasher, waiter, busboy and cook. "I got in a fight with the head chef one day, who was sort of an old drunk Marine sergeant, and he yelled at me to get out of his kitchen. Tom Caine, the manager, told me to apologize, and I said, 'I ain't doing it.' I walked next door to Dave, and he says, 'Come in tomorrow morning at 8.'"

It was 1967 when Frank joined Dave, Slick Spaur and Jack Leffingwell, who had taken over Leffingwell's in Brighton when his father died in 1944, then came to work for McGuckin after selling the business in 1961.[39] Frank wouldn't fully retire from McGuckin's for nearly four decades.

Bill's inventory was wide, but not exactly deep, including house and kitchenwares, high-quality Lowe Brothers paint, top-of-the-line Mercury outboard boat motors, Motorola radios, guns and ammunition, fishing tackle and licenses, and, at Dave's prompting, an assortment of tools, pipe, fittings, nuts, bolts, and other hardware.

The store couldn't afford to do much advertising, but did get some press here and there, including a small feature in the April 5, 1958, edition of Hardware World that focused on Bill's strategy of persuading customers to use their change to buy another item or two.[40]

McGuckin survived its first five years, providing a modest living for Bill and Leo, though John Valentine certainly had nothing to worry about just yet. "We did about as much business in a year back then as we do now on a slow day," Dave says.

But the city was rapidly changing, and there clearly was room for competition. With a population of 19,999 in 1950, Boulder would surge to nearly 38,000 over the next decade. President Dwight Eisenhower gave the city its first presidential visit on Sept. 14, 1954 — the next wouldn't come until 2008 — for the dedication of the new branch of the National Bureau of Standards (now the National Institute of Standards and Technology). The Boulder-Denver Turnpike opened in 1952, charging a 10-cent toll at

Broomfield and enabling commuters who didn't want to live in the city. The Rocky Flats plant opened just south of town in 1951; Ball Brothers Research Corporation became the first tenant of the Chamber of Commerce's Boulder Industrial Park in 1957; and in 1959, Beech Aircraft's Aerospace Division built a campus on 1,500 acres of land just north of the city limits to test cryogenic systems that would help develop liquefied hydrogen and oxygen rocket fuels for the Gemini space project.[41] In 1960, the I.M. Pei-designed National Center for Atmospheric Research began operations up on Table Mesa under the directorship of Walter Orr Roberts.

"All of these firms brought people from other parts of the country to settle in Boulder; most hired Boulder residents as well and were the 'clean' businesses that Boulder craved," writes historian Phyllis Smith.[42] And all those incoming residents needed hardware.

So when AMAX killed the mining community of Climax, leaving Bill's daughter, son-in-law and three young grandsons with no place to go, he knew what to do: "He called us up and said, 'Why don't you come down to Boulder and go into business with me?'" Dave says.

In October 1960, Dave, just 29, and Dee, packed up the boys and the few remnants of their brief mountain adventure to start life anew on the verge of mountain and plains. It was, to steal a line from Humphrey Bogart in "Casablanca," the beginning of a beautiful business partnership.

CHAPTER SIX

Next Door to the Lamp Post

That business really couldn't support two families. ... It was rough times.
— Dee Hight, on McGuckin Hardware in the 1960s

Dave and Dee bought a single-wide trailer and moved the family into a trailer court just off Valmont Road, and went to work at the store alongside Bill, Jack and Slick. Dee could "sell you a left-handed monkey wrench and a bastard file" — you won't find either in even the most comprehensive hardware store. And Dave? Well, he was great with customers, and he just couldn't help but offer his input on how to make the store go and grow. The first thing on his agenda was to shake the older man loose of his conservative ideas about inventory.

"We'd get a call for three-inch pipe fittings and I'd ask him, 'Bill, why don't we have these?' He'd answer, 'Dave, do you realize for one assortment (of fittings) it's $5,000?'" Dave says. "I guess I drove Dee's dad a little bit crazy. Bill always bought until he figured he'd reached his limit for the month, then quit. My thought was, let's stock it, we can either borrow the money, or in those days, a lot of the suppliers would carry you."

At Leffingwell, Dave had seen the magic of responding to customer needs, first and foremost. So if a McGuckin's customer asked for something the store didn't have, Dave wouldn't order one, but two. And if those sold, next time he'd order four, or 10. Keeping a large inventory has its costs, including taxes and storage, but Dave knew it served customers, who quickly learned that, as the 1970s-era McGuckin motto would have it, "If we don't have it, you don't need it."

"Dave's philosophy has always been to have the items in the store," says Frank Hanks, who became manager of the store in 1969. "We always carried this four-foot pipe wrench, we always had one, and we'd sell one about every five years. But when that one customer would come in looking for a four-foot pipe wrench, they'd usually buy a whole lot of other stuff."

"Dave was all about having stuff nobody else carried," says Joann Hanks, who started at McGuckin's the same year as her soon-to-be husband, Frank.

Dave also insisted on maintaining excellent personal relationships with sales reps, suppliers and jobbers. They'd never sell you something your customers wouldn't want, and in turn, you might scratch their backs, agreeing to buy and promote good products, even work with suppliers to bring in new retailers. He even developed a friendly relationship with Boulder's 800-pound hardware gorilla, John Valentine. "We always got along. I thought he was a nice guy," he says. (Note: Talk to Dave Hight for any length of time, and you soon learn that he's reticent to offer a discouraging word about anyone. When he does, he's mild about it, but rest assured that the target *really* made him mad at some point).

The store didn't have much of an advertising budget, but Dave made sure to read the Daily Camera and listen to KBOL radio for Valentine's ads. Whatever the big dog was promoting that week, he made sure to stock at McGuckin's.

But the little upstart on Arapahoe was struggling to get by.

"That business really couldn't support two families at the time," Dee says. "It was rough times."

Bill's experience with oil-lease auctions made him a shrewd bargainer, and in 1963 he won an auction for 20 acres of land across from Bald Mountain in Sunshine Canyon west of Boulder. The Hights had the trailer home hauled up the hillside, and with the help of two local cowboys, Warren Slatendale and Dale Simms(Dave and Dee may not be ranch people, but there is a fine, rich vein of cowboy wit and wisdom running throughout McGuckin's history) Dave started building a house. Self-taught while building the family's house in Brighton, and displaying the attitude that would be instilled in generations of McGuckin's employees, Dave pounded nails, sawed boards, put in heating ducts and plumbing and wired the whole thing — you do whatever it takes to get the job done.

The house was also a learning opportunity for the boys, Brent, Barry and Robb. By the time they were 10 years old, Dave was teaching his sons how to pull wire, put in electrical sockets and even install a hot water heater in the crawlspace with a soldering torch.

During the 1960s, "We were sweating joints" — using a torch to join copper pipes with tin solder — "not smoking them," Barry deadpans.

In 1965, after three and a half years living in a trailer, the family was living in a house once again. It wasn't fancy, just a wood-frame affair with a living room, kitchen, utility room, two bedrooms and two bathrooms, and a porch, but it sure had a spectacular view of the plains stretching away east. Money was still scarce, so the family ate simply — peanut-butter sandwiches for lunch and "scroodles," corkscrew noodles (no one knew the word "pasta," much less "fusilli") with hamburger and tomato sauce for dinner — and Dee baked all their bread. The boys worked in the school lunchroom for their lunches, and Dee used her old sewing skills to keep clothes from going to pieces as long as possible. They had a phone, but it was on the Sunshine Canyon party line.

The boys started attending school at Washington Elementary on north Broadway, and later, Mapleton Elementary, in the heart of one of the city's oldest and most exclusive neighborhoods. Even then it was home to the wealthy and powerful, including Republicans U.S. Rep. Don Brotzman and Colorado Gov. John Love, who maintained a second house on Mapleton. (Though unimaginable to many latter-day Boulderites, the town was conservative, quiet and frankly Midwestern, and elected mostly Republicans until the tail-end of the 1960s, when it began to grow into its current incarnation as one of America's true liberal bastions).

Business owners or not, "We were mountain people," Dee says, "so people didn't like us going through the Mapleton neighborhood. They didn't want any mountain trash."

But up in Climax, the family had developed a healthy, Wild West streak, and life on the mountain suited them. The boys rode horses, scouted the nearby canyons and played baseball with kids from nearby Sunshine, a former mining town turned sleepy hamlet.

Dave did just about everything at the store, selling, buying, ordering and stocking, and Dee had gradually become the bookkeeper for the business. She'd type up billing statements on an aging manual typewriter and lay them out on her living-room floor in alphabetical order, a setup constantly threatened by boys charging in and out.

"I'd holler for them to close the door, don't make waves, or else the wind would blow everything all over," Dee says.

The boys were given the unenviable task of licking every envelope.

"I thought we'd died and gone to heaven when we finally got a sponge and saucer," Barry says.

Dee, former sharp-eyed store detective at the Fremont Trading Post, now also found herself in the role of bill collector. She'd load the boys up in her car and drive around town, knock on delinquents' doors to hand them an overdue bill. One day, she was determined to get the owner of Westy's Garage, who had let a $25 account linger until interest had driven it up to $35.

"I saw him hauling a lot of cars, and he seemed to be doing pretty well. We weren't. So I walked up to the door, and he came out. He stood about 6'4", a huge guy, and I said, 'Mr. Westy, would you please pay your bill?'" Dee says. "Well, he looked down at me and said, 'Young lady, I will pay your bill when I'm damned good and ready. Now get off my porch.'"

"I told her, 'No more bills after that, you're going to get shot,'" Dave says. Dave hired another big man, Jack Thompson, to do collections, paying him half of whatever he could shake out of recalcitrant customers. "Half was better than nothing, and Dee didn't get shot. Let Jack get shot."

But Dave also had learned growing up that there was no shame in showing a little compassion and charity in business. John Jacobs, who farmed property at 75th Street and Arapahoe, ran up a walloping bill of around $750, more than $5,000 today, with inflation. But he had a disabled employee, and a good chunk of the bill was interest. Even Jack Thompson had been unsuccessful in getting him to pay.

"He came into the store one day feeling bad. He said, 'I'll give you $300,' and I said that would settle it," Dave says. "Of course, he came in a month later and wanted to charge again."

McGuckin's also struggled to make good on accounts run up by one of Boulder's most colorful characters from the 1930s until her death in 1987, Minnie Mae Cunningham. Living in a dank stone house on her sprawling farm at 4th and Kalmia streets, on the verge of north Boulder's dramatically rising foothills, she was better known to local kids and neighbors as "the goat lady." Since the death of her husband, Everett, in 1937, she'd scratched out a living selling eggs, chickens and goat milk, teaching school, substitute teaching and tutoring. Her small herd of goats and sleek, healthy horses grazed up and down the hillside, a pleasant pastoral scene that endured even after the surrounding area had been turned into high-end housing developments.

But the goat lady was not always pleasant herself, and tales of her firing buckshot into the scampering hindquarters of young trespassers gave her a fearsome reputation. She terrified genteel birdwatchers wandering along her hillside, and if anyone dared drive down the dusty lane connecting 4th Street to Linden Drive, she'd hike her skirt and chase after them with a shotgun. She gave the city fits, filing a suit in 1966, claiming that crews building a sewer line across her property had made her fences "un-goatworthy"; she eventually won a judgment of $16,000.[43]

But diplomatic adult neighbors managed to make her friendship and came to see her as an unappreciated, if cranky, defender of nature. By the time her barn burned in February 1975, she'd softened toward her bureaucratic nemeses at city hall and sold most of her 40 acres as open space.

"Mrs. Cunningham was a very interesting and attractive neighbor," said Kurt Gerstle, who first met her in 1959. "She had a deep affection for the land and the animals and everything around her."[44]

Minnie Mae was a frequent customer at McGuckin's, but not usually the promptly paying kind, at one point running up a bill of several thousand dollars. But Dee appreciated her fiery spirit and hired her to tutor Robb when he was 8 or 9. Nobody, but nobody — not even friendly neighbors — was ever allowed into Minnie Mae's inner sanctum, a squat, brooding stone farmhouse, so she would instruct her young student in the front seat of her old Buick (the back seat, like much of her property, was piled high with junk she'd picked up somewhere).

One day when Dee arrived to pick up her youngest from his lessons, Minnie Mae pointed to a thick-necked stallion imperiously flipping his mane and forelock as he grazed confidently on the hillside next to her goats and lesser equines.

"She said, 'That dang thing hasn't been ridden. You think Robb could ride him for me?'" Dee says.

Riding bucking horses is tough enough when they're geldings or mares; a stallion is prone not just to buck an irritating rider off his back, but to turn around and do a little hoof-dance on a dismounted bronc-buster's face. All the Hight boys were riders, but cowboy Wilber McGuckin's bronc-riding blood ran reddest in Robb's veins. The boy had always taken to Slick Spaur, the rangy cowboy who worked at the store and schooled him in how to stay aboard a wild, leapin' cayuse. Whenever he did get bucked off, Robb followed Spaur's advice and got right back on, and he relished riding bulls at the Little Britches rodeo in Boulder's popular annual Pow Wow.

"I guess I don't care," Dee told Minnie Mae with a shrug. "Ask Robb."

Young Robb would be obliged, thank you. He not only rode the big stallion, but tickled his tutor to death with his cowboy bravado.

"Robb just jammed the stallion up against the corral and climbed on, no bridle, saddle or anything," marvels his older brother, Barry.

Minnie Mae never did make good on her McGuckin bill. Dave wrote it off after she moved to Boulder Manor care facility, where she died in 1987.

Curious kids (and, rumor has it, even some adults) couldn't resist sneaking into to the old stone house after she departed, finding it stuffed with curiosities and wonders, from long racks of elegant evening dresses to endless rows of dusty Ball jars, still holding pickles made a half-century earlier, and stacks of yellowed newspapers. The house, outbuildings, and all their contents were bulldozed in 1993.

"She probably owed the store $5,000 or $6,000 bucks, but by then she was in a home. So we just wrote it off," Dave says.

In 1965, the same year Dave and Dee moved up the mountain, the owners of Thunderbird Square, Boulder's newest shopping center, on the southwest corner of Baseline Road and what is now Colorado Highway 157, or the Foothills Parkway, approached McGuckin's about opening a satellite store in a 3,000-square-foot space, alongside Thunderbird Cleaners and Laundry, a Safeway store, a new branch of Anderson Drug, Thunderbird Beauty Salon and three other businesses.[45] Dave and Bill hadn't been planning to expand, but the thought of capturing the business of thousands of south Boulder residents — the sprawling Frasier Meadows subdivision had been platted in 1958 and nearby Martin Acres in 1959 — suddenly seemed to make sense.

They decided to bite, but since Bill was doing most of the buying at the store while Dave ran the front end, worked the sales floor and, with help from Dee, handled billing, payroll and accounting, they sent their resident cowboy, Slick Spaur, out to run the place. Bill also decided it would be good for business if McGuckin's joined the Ace Hardware co-op.

"I didn't know a lot about co-ops at the time," Dave says, "and we just treated them as another wholesaler."

McGuckin's paid $4,000 for the privilege (about $28,000 in 2015 dollars) and getting good prices on merchandise bought through the Ace co-op, and in theory, the store was supposed to buy much of its stock from Ace. But the co-op's nearest warehouse was in Chicago, which didn't exactly fit in with Dave's philosophy of meeting customers' needs as quickly as possible. After Bill died, Dave just didn't order that much from Ace. A few years later he got a call from a bigwig in Chicago, who upbraided him for buying only about $35,000 worth of inventory from the co-op in the last year.

"I said, 'That surprises me.' He says, 'What?' 'That I bought that much!'" Dave says, chuckling. "I said, 'Your service is terrible. I'm used to ordering something and getting it in a few days, not three months later.'"

The Ace man was not amused. He started a lecture about loyalty.

"I'm used to people earning my loyalty," Dave interrupted, "not calling me up on the phone telling me I have to be loyal."

The man threatened to take McGuckin's franchise away.

"Oh really?" Dave shot back. "Why don't you cram your franchise up your ass and see if it makes your eyes bulge?"

The next day he and Frank Hanks packed up remaining Ace inventory in a big box and shipped it to Chicago, freight-collect.

"I never did get that $4,000 back," Dave says with a shrug, but it's clear he thinks that was an acceptable price for the opportunity to cuss out that Chicago bigwig.

The Thunderbird "mini McGuckin's" was just barely holding its own, but business at the main store continued to grow right along with the community. By the time IBM had opened its huge new campus between Boulder and Longmont in 1965, an influx of new population growth spurred Boulder over 50,000 for the first time and sent it galloping toward nearly 67,000 residents by 1970, encouraged by local government policies. The city even agreed to construct a new water treatment plant near Boulder Reservoir to sweeten the pot when IBM first came sniffing around.

"The Jaycees" — the Boulder chapter of the U.S. Junior Chamber — "and especially Paul Crouch of Crouch Motors was instrumental in getting IBM to come here," Dave says. "Paul could sell refrigerators to the Eskimos, and he was the one who got the water line."

The growth in population and employment in the mid-'60s precipitated a housing construction boom, and the city began platting new subdivisions with names like Heatherwood and Gunbarrel Green just minutes away from the IBM plant. And all that building, all those new residents, translated into soaring demand for hardware and construction goods.

But with growth and opportunity came new competition, as well. Local officials and most residents were thrilled when Texas developer Gerri von Frellick built the 400,000-square-foot Crossroads Shopping Center on county land just east of 28th Street in 1963.[46] The flat, sprawling edifice cashed in on a nationwide craze for indoor shopping malls and attracted natural McGuckin's competitors such as Montgomery Ward, J.C. Penney and the Denver Dry Goods Company, as well as smaller local shops, a food court and a multi-screen movie theater.

"I've always said that if not for IBM we might not be here," Dave says. "Crossroads had gone in and sucked business away from downtown and from us. When that (IBM) payroll hit Boulder, and they started buying houses in Frasier Meadows and Heatherwood, it really saved a lot of businesses that were in trouble."

As if Crossroads weren't enough, 1965 presented further challenges when Kmart and Woolco opened huge new discount stores over on 28th Street.

"They definitely took some business away, especially in housewares and containers," Dave says. "But I never felt they were out to put you out of business."

He could not say the same for Gibson's Discount Center, which opened a giant new store, just as boxy and utilitarian as the new mall or Kmart, at the corner of 28th Street and the Diagonal Highway. Started in Little Rock, Arkansas, in the 1930s by "modern discount retailing pioneer" Herbert Richard Gibson, the company was an early rival that was said to have influenced the management strategy of Walmart founder Sam Walton. Despite battling constant antitrust lawsuits challenging its purchasing and distribution procedures, Gibson's was a billion-dollar company and boasted more than 400 stores nationwide when the Boulder store opened. With Walmart yet to peak, Gibson's stated ambition was to surpass Kmart and Sears as the nation's top retailer.[47]

Dave immediately recognized Gibson's as a different kind of threat. He'd competed amiably with Boulder's hardware giant, Valentine's, for years, but this company was out to destroy competition altogether. Able to buy in huge quantities direct from factories, Gibson's could also afford drastic price-cutting to hook shoppers and "footballing" on top product lines, selling goods such as Coleman fuels and Stanley Thermos bottles for way below market price, to get people in the door. The company seemed uninterested in supporting families or family-owned manufacturers, suppliers and distributors, sending teenage employees into McGuckin's to write down prices in order to mark their version of the product way down.

"When Gibson came to town it was a big shift. Gibson's was where Sam Walton got all his ideas, and his idea of doing business is to drive the other guy out of business," Dave says. "A lot of little towns really got hurt by them."

Unfortunately for independent businesses across the nation, Gibson's and Kmart were only in the vanguard of a trend toward corporate consolidation and market domination that would continue to expand throughout the 20th century and into the 21st.

CHAPTER SEVEN

Sole Proprietors

They told me they had a section that repaired ducks — and why not? ... It was
McGuckin Hardware, and they could do anything.

— Mark Whitehouse, on bringing an injured
bird into the store as a boy in 1970

In February 1966, Bill McGuckin badly injured the nerves in his neck
when a woman ran into him while he was skiing. He survived, but to his
only daughter, he was never the same again. In June, he was diagnosed with
lymphoma. He underwent surgery to remove the cancerous glands and endured
a long, uncomfortable course of radiation treatment, but Bill quickly recognized
the seriousness of his cancer.

"He was a pharmacist; he just knew. He wasn't sick too long, just four
months, but it was pretty bad," Dee says.

Llewellyn Commodore "Bill" McGuckin died Nov. 2, 1966. He was just
58 years old. He left behind his wife, Leo, son Ron, Dee and his grandchildren.

Bill had launched and made a decent living from the two McGuckin's,
but the business never really took off. Shortly after Bill's death, Dave and
Dee bought out her mother's shares in the store, becoming sole owners and
proprietors of a business for the first time just as Boulder, the nation and the
world were experiencing paroxysms of social, cultural and political change of a
kind unseen in their lifetimes.

The next year, 1967, would prove pivotal, as Boulder began the transition
from a quiet, generally conservative, Midwestern small town to a bastion
of liberal politics and innovative — if not controversial — approaches to
preserving the environment and the area's natural beauty. That year, Boulder
became the nation's first city to approve a tax for the purchase of "open space"

— undeveloped, natural lands — to buffer the city from development, preserve ecosystems and provide an outlet for recreation. Combined with the "blue line" — a 1959 ordinance that created a boundary and contour line that effectively prevented building above 5,750 feet of elevation in the city's mountain backdrop — the new open-space program placed Boulder in the forefront of a rising national environmental consciousness.

Also in 1967, Boulder entered a period of radical social and political transformation when voters overwhelmingly voted to jettison 60-year-old "blue laws" that prevented the sale of alcohol within city limits, 34 years after the end of federal Prohibition.

Nationally, the war in Vietnam had begun to dominate front pages by the time of Bill McGuckin's death. President Lyndon Baines Johnson, who had taken office following the shocking assassination of President John F. Kennedy on Nov. 22, 1963, was elected in a landslide election over Republican Barry Goldwater in 1964, in part because of Johnson's perceived willingness to de-escalate U.S. involvement in a distant war in which Kennedy had embroiled the nation. But on Aug. 2, 1964, based on what would turn out to be the much-exaggerated Gulf of Tonkin incident, Johnson persuaded Congress to allow him to "take all necessary measures to repel any armed attack against forces of the United States and to prevent further aggression." In early 1965, the first American combat troops arrived in Vietnam, and the U.S. began a sustained bombing of North Vietnam that would continue for three years. By 1967 there were nearly a half-million U.S. troops in Vietnam — up from 23,000 just three years earlier — and unrest began to make the front pages of newspapers and TV newscasts almost daily.

Just like the earlier Lost Generation following World War I, and the Beat Generation after World War II, in the late 1960s a new wave of disillusioned, mostly white, middle-class, young people began to seek out life's pleasures in the most beautiful places they could find, and Boulder was a natural destination for these so-called "flower children," who were "taking a vacation from society."[48]

"They hitchhiked into town carrying a sleeping bag and a few belongings on their backs, or came in colorful but untidy vans. Most were bedraggled and dirty but seemingly free from the shackles of the 'straight' society of their parents," writes historian Phyllis Smith. "Hitchhiking, sleeping overnight in cars in front of Boulder residences, panhandling, jaywalking and open use of drugs — all these activities enraged many Boulderites."[49] City leaders were so concerned that they closed Central Park and declared it a public health hazard.

The war, the hippies and campus activism didn't coalesce into the kind of public demonstrations and unrest seen in other cities until 1970, when CU students began to skip classes to attend marches and, in April, occupy Regent Hall. But the city as a whole was still in transition, and voters narrowly rejected a referendum that fall that would have notified President Richard Nixon and Congress of Boulder's disapproval of their policies and the war in Southeast Asia. Things turned violent in 1971, when three days of rioting resulted in broken windows and looting on University Hill, kicking off sporadic anti-war protests over the next two years. Responding to Nixon's mining of Haiphong Harbor in North Vietnam in May 1972, for example, thousands of CU students blocked traffic on U.S. 36 — the Denver-Boulder Turnpike — at Baseline Road with barrels, concrete barriers and firewood, setting fires and throwing rocks and bottles.

E.C. Pickett Loan took out sardonic advertisements reflecting the opinion of many business owners and city residents: "Our mayor says he's 'disappointed' over the Uni-hill riot. Goodness, gracious, golly, gee! Shouldn't he stop using such strong language over mere looting, assault and arson?" Another Pickett ad read, "Peacenik roadblocks didn't inconvenience radical CU profs, who can cancel classes as they please without penalty. It was the hourly-paid working man who was the innocent victim."[50]

Some McGuckin's employees knew all about that. Barry Hight remembers one night as a teenager when he and store employee Irving Sandvold — a crusty Norwegian born in 1906 whose personal motto was, "Dave vants you to vork, so you vork!" — got caught up in a wave of protesters. Irv had driven with Barry in a company truck up to a rented storage site in a two-story garage on University Hill to unload a semi-truck full of fertilizer and return to the store with shovels, rakes, hoes and other gardening equipment. Returning via a roundabout route because of street protests, Irv nevertheless had to come to a stop at the intersection of 28th and Arapahoe as a mob of anti-war protesters surged around the truck.

"We are the first car in line, and we can't get through. I just looked like a kid with my grandpa with me, and when the light turns green Irv just leans on the horn and yells that he's late for work. The sea just parted," Barry says, laughing. "After we got through I said 'Irv, goddamn, I thought we were going to get mugged.' It would have been like 'Frankenstein' — we had all the implements right there in the truck."

But as the rolling unrest spilled out across the city, the situation didn't look particularly amusing to business owners. Protesters broke windows at the military recruiting office in Arapahoe Village and were throwing rocks at cars trying to flee the mayhem. Dave decided he had no choice but to sit sentinel in front of the store with a loaded .22-caliber rifle for a few nights.

"They were breaking windows all over town, turning police cars over. I really thought they were going to burn the store down," he says. "I support people demonstrating for a good cause and exercising free speech, but they shouldn't destroy property. If you're in the retail business, that can really hurt you."

But as instability and seismic change rocked Boulder in the late 1960s and into the early '70s, McGuckin Hardware was growing and laying stable foundations — of people, practices and philosophy — that would last into the next century.

Frank Hanks, who had asked Dave Hight for a job after he was canned from the Lamp Post in 1967, started with no experience in sales or hardware. He'd grown up in Laramie, Wyoming, where his father worked for the Safeway grocery store chain, moved to Boulder in 1965, then graduated from Denver's Ranum High School before taking the restaurant job. Frank was early proof that Dave had an eye for hard workers and wasn't afraid to train a good prospect.

"I was the new kid on the block, of course," Frank says. "Dave taught me everything I know."

Rule number one? Make sure you have what people want. Poring over supplier and distributor catalogs that could be literally a foot thick was fun, but ultimately, the best way to find out what to put on the shelves was to listen to customers. Everybody at McGuckin's was stationed at the front of the store, so they could greet customers the minute they walked in, stay with them right through the sale and help carry items out to their cars.

"If you tell somebody you want to help them, help them. But don't give them any bullshit," Frank says, summing up Dave Hight's earthy humility. "I learned from Dave: Don't be afraid to tell them you don't know something. They will train you. They will help you."

Frank retired in 2006, but says Dave's lessons will go with him to the grave: "I can't go into a store today and see someone who's not being waited on. I get nervous as hell, start looking around — what's wrong? Why isn't someone waiting on them?"

Protesters may have been making headlines, but there was still a fair dose of "old Boulder" left when Frank started. Almost unimaginable to anyone who arrived after 1975, in the late '60s the city still had its share of miners, prospectors, ranchers, farmers, cowboys and other colorful relics of its frontier past. Even before John B. Valentine sold the business his father joined in 1906 — in 1970, to two Chicago investors who ran it into the ground after two years, leaving the Boettcher Building without a hardware tenant for the first time since 1873 — McGuckin's had become the supplier of choice for many old-timers.

Guys like George Poor, a ditch-rider on the Farmer's Ditch and muleskinner who hauled lumber out of the mountains, and Bill Berryman, a stove-up, old farrier who bought horseshoes and sold pry bars and tamping bars to Dave for cash.

"Jack (Leffingwell) didn't want to sell the horseshoes, because they were so dirty. I got all the dirty jobs," Frank says. "Bill would only deal with Dave for a long time, but after awhile he'd let me deal with him, and we became good friends. The first time I sold him horseshoes I said, 'You want two?' Bill looked right at me and said, 'How many feet does a horse have on it?'"

When Frank came aboard, "Valentine's was still *the* hardware store in Boulder," he says. Dave still couldn't afford to advertise much, but piggybacked off his competitor's big weekly ads, making sure he had whatever items Valentine's was pitching that week. Jim Kithcart, an advertising rep from Russ Shaffer's KBOL, seemed to be in the little guy's corner, promising Dave that radio advertising would "make McGuckin the hardware name in Boulder, so when people think hardware, they'd think McGuckin."

Frank was still young, and he figured he'd work at the store for a year or two, tops, before moving on to construction or something else. But it didn't take long for him to develop loyalty to Dave, "who was like a father to me, still is. He knew me better than my own father." Plus, he was being paid well and got to go home at 5 p.m. and had Sundays off. But one night as he walked out the door, Frank asked Dave who handled the night work of stocking, pricing and cleaning up.

"He said, 'I do.' 'By yourself?' I asked. Well, I didn't think that was right, so I started staying and working nights with him," Frank says.

It didn't take too long for Frank to ask the next obvious question: Who works Sundays? Dave again. By himself. Frank didn't think that was fair, either, and started showing up Sundays, too.

"We worked seven days a week, sometimes 12 or 13 hours a day," he says. "But I didn't mind; Dave and Dee treated me so well."

One night as they were marking orders, Dave started feeling guilty that he was overworking his loyal night employee. He turned and said, "Hey Frank, I'm tired. Let's go home." So they cleaned up, snapped off the lights, left through the back door, locked up and got in their cars. But by the time he hit Canyon Boulevard and 15th Street, Dave couldn't stand it; there was just too much work to do for him to be going home "early." He turned around and drove back to the store.

"When I got to the back door, here's Frank standing there. He says, 'I knew you were going to do that,'" Dave says. So he unlocked the door, and they both went back to work. "Hell, once Frank came to work for me I couldn't drive him off."

The store's fifth full-time employee was Harry T. "Ran" Ransom, who, like Frank, would stay with the store right into the new century, along with Earl Duncan, who joined the company in 1974, Bruce Ramp (1971) and John Haskovec (1975). Ran graduated from Boulder High School in 1961 and was working for Hoke Johansen's hardware on north Broadway when Dave ran into him in a tire shop. Trusting his gut, he told Frank to hire Ran immediately if he ever came around looking for a job. He did, on June 22, 1969, and stayed on until cancer forced his retirement in 2014.

"There was only one Ran Ransom, that's for sure," Dave says. "His dream was about the same as mine, and that was to build a really outstanding hardware store."

A fixture on the floor for 45 years, Ransom epitomized the celebrated McGuckin's tradition of invention, innovation and ingenuity and making the store a genuine partner with countless inventors and entrepreneurs over the years. He was forever brainstorming with customers and tailoring solutions to whatever was vexing them, his mind snapping through ideas like a playing card going *brrrrrap* across some kid's bicycle spokes.

"He would definitely always have an opinion or an answer or a solution, or he would make something up. He'd say, 'I don't know. Let's try it. Let's open it up,'" says Randy "Doc" Dilkes, who joined McGuckin's in 1978 and is now the store's longest-serving manager. "He wouldn't want to work on anything unless he knew all about it. A total inventor, take-it-apart kind of guy."[51]

The store's first non-family female employee came aboard in August 1968, replacing a secretary who "did everything," but had just quit. Joann Papini grew up just a few blocks from McGuckin's in Boulder's Goss-Grove neighborhood and had just graduated from Boulder High School. Her brother Dave, who would later own and operate Dave's Tonsorium barbershop on north Broadway for many years, knew Frank Hanks from his job at the Lamp Post.

"I was 12 when I met Frank," says Joann. "We were engaged when I was 16, and I was married three weeks out of high school. Frank was almost late for our wedding because he couldn't get out of work at the store. … When I started I was just a kid, and Dave scared me, though he's really not gruff at all. I guess it all worked out."

It did indeed.

LEFT: Dee Hight as a child.

FAR LEFT: Dave Hight seen in a school photo from 1939.

ABOVE: Dee feeds Dave a piece of their wedding cake in the fall of 1950.

LEFT: "Hights cut cake in traditional manner" reads the Society and Club News headline, depicting Dave and Dee cutting their wedding cake at Bill and Leo McGuckin's house in the fall of 1950.

I

TOP: Brent, left, Barry, Dave and Robb Hight in July 1959.

ABOVE LEFT: Barry, left, Brent and Robb Hight, somewhere in Boulder circa 1977 with Brent's 1975 Porsche 911.

ABOVE RIGHT: Dee Hight, left, her brother Ron McGuckin, and parents Leo and Bill McGuckin stand in front of the family automobile in Fort Lupton in 1951.

RIGHT: Brent, left, Dee, Robb and Barry Hight pose with Flicka the family dog in 1965.

ABOVE: "Bill invites you to come in and see his full line of Hardware-Sporting Goods-Grass Seed" in the first advertisement promoting the opening of McGuckin Hardware on Sept. 9, 1955.

LEFT: Bill McGuckin makes a transaction at the store's original location at 2635 Arapahoe Avenue in Boulder.

ABOVE: Dave Hight and his father-in-law, Bill McGuckin, stand in front of the store's original location in the early 1960s.

RIGHT: A look at the register at the store's original location at 2635 Arapahoe Avenue.

BELOW RIGHT: Inside the store's original location at 2635 Arapahoe Avenue.

BELOW: The front of the McGuckin satellite location in the Thunderbird Square Shopping Center (circa 1965).

ABOVE: Bill McGuckin, pictured behind the "O," stands behind a sign commemorating the grand opening of the Thunderbird Square Shopping Center in 1965.

LEFT: A joint advertisement from the Dec. 15, 1965, edition of the Daily Camera promoting the opening of Thunderbird Square.

BELOW LEFT: Harry "Ran" Ransom at the register at the Thunderbird store circa 1969.

BELOW RIGHT: Storefront of McGuckin Hardware's satellite location, aka "Mini-McGuckin," in Thunderbird Square, featuring a Scott's Turf Builder banner.

RIGHT: One of the first ads for the Boulder Ski Deals location in 1973. Bruce Ramp, upper left, mixes red paint to match a chunk of rock from the Flatirons brought in by the city after vandals painted the large, white "CU" letters on the Third Flatiron. Dave Hight, upper right and bottom, merchandising the paint department and tool department, respectively.

BELOW: The original McGuckin Hardware logo and slogan.

Make McGuckin Hardware your one-stop for home improvement supplies. In our new location we have a separate department for hardware, houseware, paint and garden supplies. This is to enable fast, convenient shopping for our customers. Each department is stocked with every known item possible. We're noted for our complete stock of merchandise & good service. At McGuckin, we work for you!

McGuckin Hardware
2526 Arapahoe   443-1822

Colorado's favorite store!

mh
mcguckin hardware

ABOVE: Dave, left, and his brother Jack Hight stand with Frank Hanks in front of the Boulder Ski Deals location on Jan. 8, 1974.

RIGHT: An original mock-up of the "MH" icon, designed by Lori Hight (Brent Hight's wife) when she attended art school at Colorado State University (1976-78).

ABOVE: The McGuckin Hardware Green Machine won the honors of "Best Engineered" craft in the 1980 Kinetics competition. The team, from left, included Glenn Mason, Sue Wiggins, Lynn Glinsky (Mann), Ed Regal Sr., Jon Dunwell, Tim Fremgen, Ken Phillips, Frank Hanks, Robb Hight, Todd Hornby and Brian Athearn. Part of the Alpine Chevron entry can be seen at left; it was built from an old Vail gondola cabin.

ABOVE: The McGuckin Motion Commotion II Kinetics entry — the exact year is unclear — parked outside the now-east entrance of the store facing what is now the Marriott.

RIGHT: Harry "Ran" Ransom, left, and Bruce Ramp in the garden department at McGuckin Hardware's second location, which now houses Boulder Ski Deals. Arapahoe Avenue can be seen through the window in the background. Ran and Bruce grew their hair and beards out to mark America's bicentennial celebration in 1976.

ABOVE: The store's current location was expanded to the east, seen during that construction in 1991 or 1992. Here, heavy machinery prepares the foundation in the foreground for what will eventually become the Marriott Hotel's parking garage; McGuckin Hardware's current location is under construction in the background.

ABOVE: Dave Hight walks through the construction site of McGuckin Hardware's current location in 1977.

RIGHT: Virginia Cohagen, left, Reg Platts, Dave Hight and John Cohagen Jr. stand in front of the south entrance of the 2525 Arapahoe Avenue store during the location's grand opening on Oct. 19, 1978.

BELOW RIGHT: Shoppers peruse McGuckin's wares in the west end of the store before the 1992 expansion. Seen here are the sporting goods and garden departments, with housewares in the background. Look closely to the bottom right and you can see the blue-and-yellow roller skates that were popular at the time. On the left, cashiers hand-write out charges; credit charges were imprinted on carbon forms. To the far left, Bill Ekrem, housewares buyer, walks through the store.

TOP: This trio of McGuckin cashiers shows off their Halloween costumes at the north registers. The photo is thought to be from around 1986.

ABOVE: Facing west from Dave's office over the builder hardware department before the expansion. This photo was taken from the east-most wall before it was knocked down as part of the 1992 expansion.

ABOVE: Dick Pay, left, discusses fire starters with Kenny Phillips in the fireplace accessories aisle in 1978.

RIGHT: Customers wait in the checkout line.

BELOW RIGHT: Looking east down an aisle inside the store's 2525 Arapahoe location circa 1980. Yes, that is a disco ball hanging from the ceiling.

ABOVE: McGuckin Hardware's west entrance is illuminated at night in 1977.

BELOW: Don Glinsky, left, Dave Hight, center, and Rik Isakson goof off at the 2525 Arapahoe location.

Business Plus

DAILY CAMERA   Tuesday, April 23, 1991   SECTION D

KEEPING BOULDER IN GOOD REPAIR

McGuckin Hardware's motto: 'If we don't have it, you don't need it'

By SHAWN WAGGONER
For the Camera

Most businesses are thinking about customer service these days, but at least one Boulder business, McGuckin Hardware in The Village Shopping Center, has it nailed down.

More that just a nuts-and-bolts kind of place, McGuckin's stocks an amazing range of housewares, building supplies, sporting goods and appliances, just to name a few categories. Customers say they can find anything they need among McGuckin's 300,000-item inventory, from the most basic supply item to the most unusual piece of something or another.

Some of McGuckin's prices may be steeper than the competition, but few of the store's customers seem to mind. It's the service — provided by those green-vested sales people that know how to find everything — that keeps the customers coming back. In all, McGuckin Hardware employs 150.

Plaques announcing "If we don't have it, you don't need it," decorate management offices on the second floor of the 42,000-square-foot store. If a product can't be found among the store's rows of 18-foot shelves, it probably can't be found anywhere, McGuckin's customers agree.

Hight, who owns McGuckin's with his wife Donna Mae and three sons, is tenaciously tight-lipped about the store's revenues, number of customer transactions yearly or dollar volume of the inventory. He said he fears giving an edge to the competition, such as home centers of discount department stores and building supply centers.

Hardware Merchandiser, a trade publication, put McGuckin's revenues at $6 million in 1989 when the store employed 100. Hight said revenues have "grown steadily" over the past several years.

Industry changes

It hasn't been easy for independently operated McGuckin Hardware to compete with chains that buy products in bulk, passing price breaks along to customers, said corporate general manager Ken Renner, a five-year employee.

Most independent hardware stores have been crowded out by competition from retail chains or have folded simply because they can't generate enough income

EUGENE TANNER / Daily Camera

HARDWARE STORE GALORE: McGuckin Hardware has built a following of customers who count on finding what they need, no matter how odd the request. McGuckin's is owned by Dave Hight, front, and sons from left, Brent, Robb and Barry.

See CUSTOMER / Page 10

Brush aside current sweepstakes scam PAGE 4	'Branching' out: Banking change afoot PAGE 5	Secretaries' Day is time to say thanks PAGE 7

ABOVE: Brent, left, Dave, Robb and Barry Hight posed in front of the store's west entrance for a story about the store that appeared in the Daily Camera's Business Plus section in 1991.

RIGHT: Outside the Power Service Center on 2845 Valmont Road.

ABOVE LEFT: Inside the Power Service Center at 2845 Valmont Road

ABOVE RIGHT: A McGuckin staffer works on an outboard engine in the Power Service Center.

ABOVE: A look at the newly built east end of McGuckin Hardware circa 1993.

LEFT: Looking toward the north façade of McGuckin Hardware during spring in the early 2000s shows the store nestled at the base of the iconic Flatirons.

RIGHT: A neon sign made in north Boulder that was legendary to locals because it was so visible from Arapahoe when McGuckin's was in the current Boulder Ski Deals location and from Folsom at the store's current location. It was the first custom neon sign created for the store. The sign became a treasured possession of the Hight family. Pictured are Brent, left, Barry, Dave, Dee and Robb Hight. This photograph was taken on Dave's 75th birthday, Dec. 8, 2007, in the McGuckin warehouse. The day included a barbecue and party with employees and friends.

ABOVE: Dave and Barry stand in front of the store's north side in March 2000.

RIGHT: A snow-frosted look up Boulder Canyon over the east end of McGuckin Hardware, taken from an upper level of the Marriott Hotel.

ABOVE: Jim Bloomer, left in front of an empty rack of sold-out of snow shovels, shows McGuckin Hardware employee Drew Paulson, right, his broken shovel on Dec. 28, 2007. Bloomer was in search of a new shovel as the second wave of heavy snow hit Boulder County and the Front Range area. The store sold 1,600 shovels and 44 snowblowers over a four-day period during the first wave of snows the prior week. *MARTY CAIVANO, DAILY CAMERA*

BELOW: Dave and Dee Hight, center, share a laugh while getting set up to be photographed with nearly 300 of their employees as part of McGuckin Hardware's 50th anniversary celebration. The business marked 50 years in 2005. *MARK LEFFINGWELL, DAILY CAMERA*

ABOVE: Al Manzi, Daily Camera publisher and CEO, right, presents Dave and Dee Hight with the 2015 Pacesetter Award in Business during the annual award ceremony at the Millennium Harvest House in Boulder on April 21, 2015.

BELOW: U.S. Rep. Mark Udall, left, presents McGuckin Hardware founder Dave Hight with a congressional citation, honoring McGuckin's for 50 years in business in the Boulder community on Oct. 14, 2005. Between Udall and Hight is employee Ken Renner. Randy Dilkes is at right. *PAUL AIKEN, DAILY CAMERA*

Joann helped Dee with the billing statements, spending hours cross-legged on the floor of the Sunshine Canyon house, ready to leap into action should an absent-minded boy open the door and let in a gremlin breeze. Soon, the two couples were working together Friday nights, marking prices on all the new merchandise and getting it on the shelves for the Saturday rush. It was a big job that often kept them in the store until after midnight.

"We called it the Friday Night Club. Joann and I would get sick of doing it after awhile; it was grueling marking all that stuff," Dee says. "We had to have a little fun, so one night she and I went to the front windows of the store and stood there as still as we could, like mannequins. People would come out of the Lamp Post and stop and stare, wondering if we were real."

Joann left in August 1970 after she became pregnant, but the couples remained fast friends, and Dee was present for the birth of all Joann's children. Joann would return when Dave found himself in a bind and needed someone to manage the office, finally retiring with Frank in 2006.

"Dave's loyalty to his employees is what makes them loyal to him. Really, it's like a family," she says. "Without that he might as well be Home Depot."

The original Friday Night Club changed a little after Ran Ransom came aboard and Joann left. Everyone at McGuckin's worked hard, but there was always a spirit of easy camaraderie.

"We're going to be working. If you want to call it the Friday Night Club then let's get a six-pack of beer," Ran told Frank and Dave, initiating a tradition that would continue for decades.

Whatever happened after dark, during the day everyone was expected to comport with the McGuckin Way — get customers in and out promptly, help out wherever you're needed and, though it wasn't as explicit, never, ever forget that everyone walking through those doors was a human being.

Mark S. Whitehouse, who lived in Boulder from 1963 to 1984, remembers a particularly poignant example of kindness. Walking to the Crossroads Mall in 1969, 9-year-old Whitehouse saw a duck fly into an electrical wire and drop like a rock. He knew exactly what to do. He scooped up the injured bird and tore across the street to McGuckin's.

"They told me they had a section that repaired ducks — and why not? After all, it was McGuckin Hardware, and they could do anything — that the duck was only shaken up, they would take care of it at no charge," Whitehouse recalls. "To this day I believe they 'repaired' the duck and it was released, good as new. … (T)he kindness that I was always shown at McGuckin is with me to this day, some 50 years later."

CHAPTER EIGHT

The passing of 'old Boulder'

We were no longer going to be the regular old hardware store.
— Frank Hanks, on McGuckin's growth in the 1970s

Bruce Ramp sees the hand of God in McGuckin's success over the years. The business has played David-with-a-slingshot almost from the beginning, managing to plant a few stones in the foreheads of some pretty daunting latter-day Philistine ogres, from Valentine's Hardware to Gibson's Discount Center, Sears and Home Depot.

"And if it weren't for God," says Bruce, who has worked as a salesman and buyer for McGuckin's for 42 years, "I wouldn't have met Dave."

Bruce graduated from CU in May 1971 into a job market his father described as "a really sorry state of affairs." He filled out dozens of applications but none of the employers even bothered to respond. Thanks to eight years of experience working at golf courses, he finally got a summer job as a groundskeeper at Flatirons Country Club on east Arapahoe. But the season wound down, and by the end of August he was laid off.

That's when Mother Nature pulled one of her signature surprises on unsuspecting Boulder (though anyone who lives in the city for long learns not to be surprised by any kind of weather, any time)as a late-summer snowstorm rolled across the Rockies on Sept. 17, dropping 18 inches of heavy snow — still a record for the month — on branches still lush with green summer foliage.

"It broke all the branches. The superintendent at the country club called me in desperation and asked if I would come back and help clean up the course," Bruce recalls. "We were supposed to use a chain saw to cut up all the limbs and stack the wood for members."

It was a big job, heavy and hard, clearing shattered limbs from towering maples, cottonwoods, elms and ash trees from 130 acres of greens, fairways and rough, then neatly stacking the sawn wood so club members could gather it for use in their winter fireplaces, and hauling the slash to the dump. To get all that done required growling chainsaws, plenty of oil and gas, wheelbarrows, heavy-duty garbage bags, tough leather gloves and more — lots and lots of hardware, in other words. The boss gave Bruce the job of shuttling back and forth to the nearest hardware store to pick up gear and supplies.

"When the chainsaws broke, or we needed oil, or another gas can, I got sent to McGuckin's," says Bruce, whose perpetual white smile and blond locks belie his 69 years.

Like many CU students before and since, Bruce had come to know and love the store, still in its original Arapahoe Village space. For a certain kind of guy or gal, it was a playground, crammed full of everything from baseball equipment and fishing tackle to hammers, light bulbs and gleaming Mercury marine engines. To Bruce, it was more than just a store. In and out of the store constantly during the cleanup project, he finally approached Dave and asked about a job.

"I don't know," Dave said. When Bruce asked for an explanation, he said, "Well, you've worked outside all your life, and I just don't know if you'll like working indoors."

"But I still want to," Bruce said. Then, not unlike a certain recently discharged Navy veteran in Norfolk, Virginia, a couple of decades earlier, he offered himself for a two-weekend tryout. At the end Dave asked Bruce if he liked the work. He did, particularly the fact that he wasn't freezing outside somewhere. But he had a question: How much did the top man at the store, manager Frank Hanks, make? The answer, $15,000 a year, or around $85,000 in 2015 dollars, seemed "like a pretty good deal" for that kind of work.

"It gave me an idea of how Dave treated his employees and what I could hope to work toward," Bruce says. "They had six employees at that point, and I told him, 'I'm going to be your lucky seven.'"

Just nine months later, Dave invited his newest employee to join him for coffee down at the Lamp Post.

"The store was just getting too big for me. So I asked him if he thought we should have departments," Dave says.

McGuckin's had grown from its original 3,500 square feet to 5,000 and now had seven employees, including Dave, so the idea made sense to Bruce. He suggested starting with a garden department, followed by fireplaces, housewares and sporting goods.

"So I turned the creation of the garden shop over to him. It was complicated, but that was all I ever had to say to Bruce and he just did it," Dave says. Once Bruce finished with that project, he moved on to the next, and the next.

"I remember after I got the garden department going, about a year and a half later, Dave wanted to know why I was buying dirt," Bruce says. "It was potting soil, for flower pots. He never criticized me, it was just, 'Do whatever you've got to do, Bruce. Let's build it, let's get it going. I always had his 100 percent support." For the next 25 years, Bruce Ramp was the architect of McGuckin's ever-expanding department structure.

One of the lucky six already working for Dave, and one of the store's most colorful characters ever, was Claire Dean "Slick" Spaur, a true cowboy throwback. Slick was born in rural Nebraska in 1926 but raised in nearby Lyons, where he hunted deer to help feed the family during the Depression.

Growing up, Slick had ridden broncs and bulls in the annual Little Britches rodeo in Boulder. After graduating from Lyons High School, the rangy cowboy spent time riding bulls on the professional rodeo circuit. But after getting busted up one time too many he went to work building houses in north Boulder with his father-in-law. One day in 1963 his friend Jim Anderson at Anderson Drug suggested he stop by McGuckin's to see if there might not be a job that was a little less taxing on his body.

"Slick was a heck of a cowboy, and all the cowboys from the national circuit used to come by and visit him," Dave says. "But he hated getting old. He knew he was going to hurt. He always said he had an extra joint in his arm, where he broke it and it was never set."

Slick advised a young Barry Hight, "Son, I broke every bone in my body ridin' broncs. Don't do it." — "And he walked like it," Barry says.

But Slick's timing was perfect.

"I was just about running the store by myself," recalls Dave, who liked to call Slick "C.D." — pronounced "Seedy" — "because Dee's dad had hurt his foot. He'd never run or even worked in a store, but I thought all that construction experience would make him a good hire."

In 1965, Dave picked Slick to run the Thunderbird mini-store. He stayed on in that job until 1973, when he retired and took to the road with his wife in an RV, wintering in Sedona, Arizona. He died a few years after McGuckin's moved into its current space in 1978, when his pacemaker failed at a Sedona restaurant that was using a microwave oven.

"He was a real cowboy, and I still use a lot of his sayings," Dave says, laughing. "When he had to urinate he'd say, 'I have to shake the dew off my lily.'"

Of course, Slick was hardly the only character around the place. Particularly in those early days, before time clocks, government-mandated overtime and sensitivity training, McGuckin's was — not that there's anything wrong with this — something of a good ol' boys club.

What else do you call a place where for a time you could settle disputes with other staff, or even an outside salesman or distributor, through boxing matches held in the parking lot after closing on Sunday? The tradition began with a housewares buyer named Mark McCrery who had a bit of a temper — after hours, he wasn't above hurling glass tumblers across the store to make a point with a recalcitrant (or simply wet-behind-the-ears) sales rep — and could sometimes rub people the wrong way. At some point, McCrery and someone else took their disagreement outside to settle it through fisticuffs. Dick Wiggins, a Townley salesman, would never let Ran Ransom forget the time he actually knocked him out.

"After that, if you got in a disagreement or personality conflict, people would say, 'Let's deal with it the way we did in school. I'll meet you Sunday after 5 in the parking lot,'" remembers McGuckin's buyer John Haskovec, who started in 1975. "But it wasn't a brawl. They used boxing gloves. And women didn't fight."

And high jinks of various kinds were practically part of the job, at least for some people. Employees raced motorbikes up and down the aisles after closing. Ran enjoyed "inventing" new products like the electric hammer — a hammer with a plug and cord attached, which sold for $15.95 — or an "ingenious" propane-to-electricity converter, nothing more than a propane tank rigged up the same way. One customer thought the electric hammer was so hilarious that he decided to tell his wife that he wanted one for Christmas.

"So she comes in and says, 'My husband wants an electric hammer.' She asked how it works, and it was, 'Just plug it in and bang, bang, bang,'" John says, smirking. "She got it for him, but she figured it out and came back in one day and said, 'You son of a bitch!'"

It wasn't as if the boss disapproved of fun. Dave Hight has been committing crimes against all that is decent and human for more than a half-century with his daily delivery of jokes to anyone who will listen: customer, employee or innocent bystander. The jests range from groan-inducing to amusing to slightly ribald to downright X-rated (though not, necessarily, actually funny). A sampling:

A man asks his psychiatrist to tell him one good thing he's gained from all the visits. The shrink takes him outside and shows him his Porsche.

When he was 16 and working for Leffingwell's, Dave told a female customer, "You can't go wrong on this mattress." To which she responded, "Well, if I can't go wrong on it, I don't want it!"

And (close your ears, kiddies): Why did the Easter Bunny hide all the eggs? Because he was f@#$%ing all the chickens!

Finally, what does RTD stand for? (Hint, according to Dave, it's not Regional Transportation District.) Raped Twice by Denver. (If you get that one, you're truly a Boulder local. It refers to the fact that Boulder citizens enthusiastically voted to tax themselves — violation one — to build a heavy-rail commuter line from Denver to Longmont, only to be told by RTD that no rail would be forthcoming — number two.)

"It's too bad Dave has never published a book of the jokes he's told," Frank Hanks says. "He always has a joke of the day. Most of them were corny. Most of the time we laughed louder than the people he told the jokes to."

After perking along just fine for nearly two decades, McGuckin Hardware finally began to really grow in the early 1970s, giving Dave and Dee the confidence to try new things. Probably the most unusual was McGuckin's venture into the manufacturing business with the Penguin Quill Spinning Wheel.

Robert M. Oliver, an engineering professor at CU, had gotten to know Dee through the store and their mutual interest in weaving. American Indian craftspeople used a drop spindle and rolling on their own legs to spin yarn, but Bob woke up in the middle of the night in 1970 with the idea to add a foot pedal to that classic design. He soon constructed a prototype, featuring large and small grooved wooden wheels mounted on a post and a foot pedal and platform underneath, so the weaver could keep the wheels spinning and her hands free.

"The Penguin Quill was really just an Indian drop spindle put to foot power," Dee says.

Bob filed for a patent on the device — later granted on March 12, 1974[52] — and contracted with McGuckin's to build them for sale. The store opened a manufacturing shop in a Quonset hut near 28th and Spruce (now home to Sports Garage) and hired Dave and Dee's oldest son, Brent, to run the operation.

Brent had wanted to go to work at McGuckin's when he was a little boy, but Dave said, "Not until you can see over the cash register." When his father remodeled the store in the early 1960s, he put in higher counters, leading his oldest son to accuse him of doing it on purpose to keep him from going to work. Now Brent had just graduated from Boulder High School, where he excelled in industrial arts, including welding and carpentry, and he was the perfect man to begin building both Penguin Wheels and other types of looms. Brent and Dee took the Penguin Wheel to craft shows as far away as Ithaca, New York, and weavers loved it. Over the next two years, Brent built and McGuckin's sold about 1,000 of them. But Bob Oliver wasn't satisfied and wanted to sell the invention to Dick Blick, an enormous art and craft supplies store started in Illinois in 1911.

"We didn't make any money on it," Dee says with a shrug. "But it was a good $190,000 education for Brent; that's what it cost us."

When Bill opened the store, Harlow Platts, founder of Western Cutlery and prominent mid-century Boulder citizen, had owned the property. His brother Reginald joined the business in 1957, but the two eventually quarreled and split the assets, with Reg taking ownership of the property and becoming Bill's first landlord.[53] By the mid-1960s, John Cohagen, who had married Reg's daughter Virginia, was managing the property. Dave got along well with his landlord, and when Haskins Pastry Shop had gone out of business in 1965, Cohagen agreed to let McGuckin's expand into that space. When Claire's Super Market finally succumbed to the arrival of King Soopers, in 1963, and Safeway — just across the street — in 1969, Cohagen tore that part of the shopping center down and allowed both the Lamp Post and McGuckin's to expand to the north, bringing the store up to about 5,000 square feet.

"Right at that time we had a really good growth spurt," Dave says, and within a couple of years McGuckin's was outgrowing its expanded space.

Parking had always been a problem at 2645 Arapahoe, even in 1960, when all the businesses in Arapahoe Village were fighting over about 40 spaces, especially during lunch and dinner at the Lamp Post. Now, with Boulder growing and business booming, the problem was even worse. But in 1973 Dave got a chance to move into much bigger quarters, just a hundred yards away.

In1973, while Dave was recuperating from back surgery — to take care of the problem first diagnosed while he was in the Navy 20 years earlier — John called and asked if McGuckin's might want to move into a new, much larger location, just across the parking lot to the west, near the Village Theater. The current tenant, Homestead House furniture store, had begun demanding that John guarantee them 18 parking spaces.

"Hell, I never saw more than three cars in front of Homestead House in all my life," Dave says.

So Dave and John shook hands on a 25-year lease on an 18,000-square-foot space that also had housed a paint store and Boulder Appliance at 2525 Arapahoe Ave., current site of Boulder Ski Deals, nearly quadrupling the size of McGuckin's. With Gibson's blown away and Valentine's now deceased, McGuckin's was now *the* pure hardware store in Boulder, Colorado.

"That was a very different store, with a big room, an upstairs, and another upstairs," Frank Hanks recalls. "We were no longer going to be the regular old hardware store."

The move put McGuckin's on the road to becoming the "everything" store it is today, and Dave was always open to suggestions from his best employees. Bruce Ramp had been busy cranking up new departments for several years already when the flashing, colored lights of a great idea went off in his head.

"I told Dave, 'The grass dies when it gets cold, the garden center is boring, we already got the automotive department started, let's do a Christmas shop,'" Bruce says. "All the garden shops would do Christmas shops in the off-season."

Dave thought it was great idea, and told Bruce to make it happen. In 1976 he dropped a 4-by-8-foot piece of plywood on two sawhorses and stocked it with a few lights, tree stands and a couple of artificial trees. It wasn't much, but customers liked it, and the next year when the grass died, Dave asked Bruce to build up the Christmas category. So Bruce put out *two* plywood-and-sawhorse displays and sure enough, they sold out. Over the next couple of decades, not only would McGuckin's become one of Boulder's favorite holiday stores — Christmas, Hanukkah, Halloween, you name it — but Bruce Ramp would travel the country year-round in search of Christmas goods, becoming something of a national legend.

"He got so good, he'd go to these shows and the buyers from all the chains would follow him around and he practically had to wear a disguise," Dave says.

Bruce rode the Christmas-buying circuit solo for a remarkable 28 years before taking on a "Santa's helper" in the mid-1990s, Marsha Haskovec, John's wife.

"We'd gone from a piece of plywood to a half-million-dollar shop, and I needed some help," Bruce says. "Marsha traveled with me, but the category is so complicated that it was five years before she took it on herself."

Marsha finally took the sleigh reins into her own hands in 2004 and has become the new Bruce, an expert in her own right. Bruce went back to selling and now works the floor four days a week, giving him more time to spend with his grandchildren.

All the changes, of course, meant a larger staff, and when the new store opened, there were 18 employees wearing green vests. By the time John

Haskovec arrived in 1975, there were 25, and the store had expanded further, building a fireplace display room in space vacated by Miller Stockman Western Wear. (Although Boulder still sported two nominally cowboy bars, Peggy's Hi-Lo out on the Diagonal and the Olympic Lounge on 30th Street, most of the customers were just slumming; about the only people who dared to wear cowboy boots and hats in public were college football fans from Oklahoma and Nebraska.)

Dave kept an office just a few minutes' walk to the east, near the old store, but he still spent most of his days on the floor.

"He worked right alongside us, and he was never 'the boss,'" says John, now the store's buyer for builder's hardware. "He didn't ever say, 'Go wait on that customer.' We were *all* there to serve the customers."

Randy "Doc" Dilkes got an unexpected, early taste of Dave's lack of ego and jack-of-all-trades philosophy. Doc moved to the area in 1976 from Philadelphia, having had enough of working for corporate home-improvement companies. He'd come for the mountains, moving to Nederland, and hoped to get a job at a sporting-goods store. Unfortunately, the only one he could find was all the way down in Denver, and a couple of snowstorms later, he knew he needed to work closer to home.

"I happened to be over at Safeway having a sandwich and sitting in the car, and I looked across the street and saw a sign for 'McGOOKins,' a sports and hardware store. I'd applied at Gart's and Dave Cook's, and I thought, 'Wow, there's a sporting goods place that isn't a corporation,' more like a mom-and-pop hardware store," Doc recalls.

He walked across Arapahoe, went in the store asked manager Frank Hanks for a job. When asked what job he was looking for, Doc smiled and said, "Well, *your* job some day." Strike one: This guy seemed to be just another East Coast newcomer with a high opinion of himself. Strike two: Doc lived in *Nederland*, home of hippies and crazy old miners and other antisocial types, and McGuckin's had not had good luck with "Ned-heads" in the past; for one thing, they tended to get stuck and couldn't come to work when it snowed; for another, they just tended to be weird. But Doc owned a Ford Bronco, a sturdy, American-made, four-wheel-drive workhorse with high clearance, and that was apparently enough for Frank to hire him on the spot for a job in the nuts-and-bolts department.

Two weeks into the job, Doc realized that the current stocking strategy of shelving hardware by manufacturer didn't make much sense in terms of customer service. Better to put all the hinges together, the cabinet hardware together, doorknobs together, like with like, rather than by manufacturer. So one day when he wasn't serving a customer, he got down on his knees and, starting with hinges, laid them out on the floor and began a full-scale rearrangement. Then he got paged to go help a customer.

"It must have taken me about 10 minutes, and when I came back, here's this guy, down on his knees, putting everything back on the shelf. I said, 'Excuse me, sir, can I help you?' 'No,' he said, 'I'm just putting these hinges back where they belong.' I explained that I was in the process of arranging them by category and he said, 'Oh, I'm sorry. I'm Dave Hight, the owner,'" Doc says. "The owner had come by and thought there was a mess going on, so he did what he'd expect any of us to do and started cleaning it up."

No sensible person actually believes that "The customer is always right" — because he isn't. But Dave always taught that his employees should treat customers with the utmost respect and courtesy, "because he's the one with the money to spend."

"We've got a good thing here at McGuckin's because of what Dave instilled in us: Take care of the customers. They are our friends, our loyal customers. They'll come back if we treat their time as valuable, get them in and get them out, give them the knowledge they want," says Earl Duncan, who started working for the store in 1974, two years after he graduated from Boulder High School, and is now back on the sales floor after working for years as a department manager and buyer.

But Dave has had a pugnacious streak since he was a boy, and isn't above challenging noisy complainers when the moment presents itself. Take the time an irate customer bashed through the doors complaining that he'd been sold a faulty maul for splitting firewood because the "rotten" handle had broken. Dave knew the problem was actually that the man had overstruck, hitting the handle instead of the maul, so he took him outside for a little demo.

"Dave took one of the mauls out to the parking lot with the guy and said, 'Let me show you something.' He hit the square edge of the curb, striking deliberately below the head, and it snapped," John says. "He looked at the guy and very calmly said, 'Hmmm. I suppose that's bad quality.'"

Some long-time employees assumed the move to the bigger store in 1973, with ever more departments and a growing staff, would inevitably erode the family atmosphere they had always loved at McGuckin's. But that didn't happen. Bruce Ramp married his wife, Tina, his college sweetheart, and in 1975 she became pregnant with their first child. When Dave found out, he didn't even bother with congratulations.

"Oh, well, we've got to pay you more then," he told Bruce. Two years later, when he found out they were pregnant again, it was the same story.

"How many people stay at a job for 40 years?" Earl says. "The Hight family always took care of us so we could raise a family, and we took care of them. As long as we did good, they did good by us."

McGuckin's employee loyalty wasn't just a matter of lip service. After moving into the new store, a new employee reported the company to federal authorities because Dave did not use an official time clock. Instead, he ran the place as he always had. People worked hard, sometimes longer hours, got paid well, and those who'd been around long enough to understand the system were not just happy, but grateful for their treatment. But labor officials conducted an audit in 1973 and ordered the store to cut checks to employees for back wages and overtime, including some as big as $7,000.

"But when he wrote the checks, most of his loyal employees wouldn't take them," Joann Hanks recalls. "They didn't want the money and knew that he was paying them better, on an hourly basis, even with overtime, on the honor system."

The officials were not amused.

"They accused me of intimidating the employees, but hell, I couldn't *make* them take the checks," Dave says. "I said, 'You go talk to 'em!' But we got that crazy clock, our first one. I couldn't run the store too well from jail, so we put in the clock."

Dave's way — the McGuckin Way — was rooted in an earlier time, an earlier ethic, what Frank Hanks calls "good old farm boy" values: Respect people and help anyone who needs help. Dee tells the story of one employee at the time who "had a little drinking problem" and ended up in jail after he'd been picked up driving on the wrong side of U.S. 36. The man jumped bail and fled to California. When he returned, Dave gave him his old job back ("We rehired him about five times," Dee says), but soon enough the law caught up with him, and he was back behind bars. Dee took cigarettes to him in jail and took the boys over to his trailer home to help clean up. The man had hardly any teeth and spent most of his money on booze. One time 11-year-old Robb had to drive his RV home because the employee was too drunk.

"Brent asked me, 'Why are we doing this?'" Dee says. "I said, 'Because it's your duty as a human being.'"

In the five years McGuckin's operated in the new, expanded location, business exploded.

"That store was so good to us," Dave says. "We did about four times the annual volume there as we did in the original store."

Yet somehow, the culture stayed the same.

"Dave and Dee would give you the shirt off their back," Frank Hanks says. "If a guy came in the store and asked for a buck for a cup of coffee, Dave would give it to him. The richest guy in the world or the poorest, they would treat them the same."

CHAPTER NINE

Reigning Champ

It was a big job. We spent four or five nights straight, working until 2 or 3 in the morning, to get everything moved.
— Randy "Doc" Dilkes, on moving to McGuckin's current site in 1978

By the late 1970s, the era of the big-box store and corporate consolidations was in full swing across America.

In 1970, Sam Walton's Walmart had become a publicly traded company, and its shares were traded on the New York Stock Exchange for the first time in 1974, the same year the company bought out its first competitor, the 16-store Mohr's chain. The company started jewelry, automotive and pharmacy divisions in 1978 — and by 1980 its 276 stores nationwide were bringing in more than $1.2 billion a year.[54]

The Target "discount store chain" opened in 1962, part of the Dayton Company, founded in 1881. In 1979, the company celebrated its first $1 billion year, reaped from just 74 giant stores in 11 states.[55]

Kmart, which grew out of the S.S. Kresge Company founded in Detroit in 1899, opened its 2,000[th] store in 1981. The company boasted a bloody history of shutting down competing retailers, including Zayre, Ames, Hill's and TG&Y and surpassed $1 billion in sales all the way back in 1966.[56]

And of course the old "department store" warhorses — Sears, Montgomery Ward, JC Penney — were still going strong.

Boulder wasn't immune to this rapidly changing economic landscape.

Though it wasn't corporate, the opening of Boulder's now-iconic Pearl Street Mall on Aug. 6, 1977, reversed years of outward commercial growth and a slowly decaying downtown, revitalizing and transforming the area into not just a place to shop, but the very heart of modern Boulder. First envisioned by architect and city planning board member Carl Worthington in 1966, construction on the four-block, red-brick outdoor mall began in June 1976.

In such an atmosphere, a family-owned outfit like McGuckin's, with its owners' quaint ideas about loyalty to employees, inventory and customer service, hardly seemed to stand a chance. The company had outlived its most established local competitor, managed — with a little help from the weather — to fend off the threat from Gibson's Discount Center and was holding its own against the Crossroads Mall, Montgomery Ward and Kmart, but would soon face a sneak attack from one of those old warhorses.

Shortly after inking the 25-year lease for McGuckin's new location, John Cohagen divorced Virginia Cohagen, leaving management of the Platt family properties to their son, John Cohagen Jr., according to Dave Hight. In 1977, without consulting him or other leaseholders, Virginia and John Jr. sold an option to Sears on the property for a reported $3 million. Sears soon sent a guy in a fancy suit, big, tall, 30-something Baron Bom, to Dave's office down by the Lamp Post to make him an offer he couldn't refuse.

Surely a little place like McGuckin's wouldn't want to have to compete with a Goliath like Sears, which *was* going in across the street, the Sears man explained reasonably. He offered to buy out the remainder of McGuckin's lease and give him a year to shut down the business. But going all the way back to scuffles on the playground in Brighton, if you wanted to get Dave Hight's hackles up, just start giving him advice he doesn't want or need. And this guy came off as kind of a punk.

"Well, that's nice of you," Dave replied coolly, "but, I've always dreamed of having a store right between you and Montgomery Ward." — which had a store at Crossroads — "You bring the traffic, and I'll sell (the customers). You guys run a terrible store; shit, you haven't even gotten into the 1930s yet!"

Three days later, agents from the Internal Revenue Service called to tell Dave he was about to be audited. They spent the next month in his office, poring over the last three years of McGuckin's tax returns in excruciating detail, "trying to put me out of business."

"But after about three days I got to be friends with those auditors, and I told 'em, 'I know Sears sent you in here,'" Dave says. "I said, 'You know, you should make Sears file tax returns on each and every location, because they move into town where there's a good retailer like me (and) just put him out of business with predatory pricing because they don't have to file tax returns. Just one for the whole damn conglomerate. And they've put a lot of my friends out of business.'"

The agents neither confirmed nor denied Dave's speculation on who pulled the strings to saddle him with a surprise audit. But a few days after they'd completed their on-site investigation, one of the agents called: "Mr. Hight, we're going to accept all your returns as filed … and I hope Sears doesn't come up there and give you a hard time."

In the end, Sears backed out of the option on the properties and opened a store in the Crossroads Mall, now long gone.

"Two hundred chain stores have come to this town and gone," Dave says defiantly. "They don't give a shit about your town. They don't think anything about closing a store down."

McGuckin's had won another round, punching above its weight, but the corporate interlopers would continue to ride into town right on into the next century, an endless succession of brawny, boastful challengers. But they only hardened Dave's resolve to do business his way, and he would eventually become one of the founding members of the Boulder Independent Business Alliance in 1998, helping to create a new model to help towns fend off homogenization and corporatization.

"McGuckin's is an exceptional story," says BIBA founder Jeff Milchen, who went on to co-found the American Independent Business Alliance in Bozeman, Montana. "So many places in America have become like clones that lack distinctive qualities, but that's something people are really looking for. You look at the cities with the strongest independent business base, the cities with stores like McGuckin's and Boulder Book Store, and they are the ones really booming right now."

Earlier in the decade, Dave had bought warehouse space on Sterling Place in east Boulder to support his approach to inventory. And not long after Sears pulled the plug on its plans for steamrolling McGuckin's, Rich Knippelmeyer, a general contractor who often worked for John Cohagen Jr. and Western Industries (formerly Western Cutlery), suggested that the shopping center already had a hell of an anchor: McGuckin Hardware. So why not act like it and build them a bigger store on the property?

Cohagen liked the idea, and work soon began on a 36,374-square-foot new building just north of the old Homestead House location. The address read 2525 Arapahoe, but the new location fit snugly between Arapahoe Avenue, Folsom Street and Canyon Boulevard, making it accessible to three major traffic arteries in central Boulder.

It also meant McGuckin's was now neighbor to a throwback business at 2460 Canyon Blvd., the southeast corner of Canyon and Folsom. Annie Joratz had operated the tattered, low-slung Joratz Motel and drive-up liquor for years, earning the eternal gratitude of local teenagers who appreciated "Granny's" relaxed attitude toward IDs. But selling booze to kids wasn't her only line, and she outraged the City Council by posting signs advertising "intimate massage" at the motel.

"She always liked me for some reason," Dave says. "I said, 'Annie, I see you're doing some advertising'"— the offending sign — "and she said, 'Yes, I've been running that same ad for years,'" Dave recalls. The motel was finally condemned in 1982, putting an end to the city's last bald-faced brothel, and Joratz died in 1988.

The new building was finished at the end of September 1978. McGuckin's closed for a week to get everything out of the old place and stock the new store. To make things easier, Dave brought in a small, propane-powered train with eight flatbed cars that ran back and forth across the parking lot alongside forklifts and employee pickup trucks.

"That was an 18,000-square-foot store, and it was a big job," Doc Dilkes recalls. "We spent four or five nights straight, working until 2 or 3 in the morning to get everything moved."

Inevitably, some merchandise remained outside, waiting to be moved, and to prevent theft, McGuckin's hired a security guard. But the man was more thief than guard himself: He waited until everyone had headed home, exhausted, then backed up his car, filled it with merchandise and took off. So Dave tried again, this time hiring a big, stern woman who took the job so seriously that she tied cans to fishing line and strung it around the property as a sort of low-tech burglar alarm. Frank Hanks stopped by one night to check things out, and the beefy woman leapt up from her lawn chair waving a wooden club and shouting, "Stop! Don't cross that line!"

"She was a big gal. She looked like a truck driver," Dee says. "We came to find out that she was a nun from the St. Walburga's convent out on Baseline Road. She looked mean, but she was actually very sweet."

The legend of McGuckin's "nun with a nightstick" was born.

On Oct. 19, 1978, the new store opened with 80 employees on the payroll. Dave unlocked the doors and walked the length of the new store with Virginia Cohagen, John Jr. and his old friend Reg Platts, who was nearing the end of his long life.

"We became the first independent hardware store to build a really big store in town," Dave says, "and it was an immediate hit."

But nobody was dumb enough to think they could now rest on their laurels.

After all, two weeks earlier, a huge national chain had painted its red target on the green vest.

Even with 80 employees, more than twice the square footage of the previous store and shelves stocked with well north of 100,000 items, Dave and Dee refused to scrap the personal, family-minded, old-school philosophy that had served them so well for so long. Dave still insisted on walking down to the floor each payday to personally hand checks to every employee, in part to be sure he knew everyone working at the store.

"For years he had 100 checks in his back pocket and he'd start in the morning, walking around. It took him all day, as he would visit people; he knew you, by your first and last name," says store manager Bob Perkins. "He'd take so long that happy hour would start rolling around at 4:30, and people would get nervous and start asking, 'Has anyone seen Dave? I need my paycheck.'"

Bob was astonished by the culture he found at McGuckin's when he hired on in October 1980. He'd worked at his grandfather's hardware store and thought he'd come to Colorado to be a ski bum. Not long after arriving in Boulder, he walked into McGuckin's and handed his resume to the receptionist, who glanced at it and sniffed, "I think we already have our quota of New Yorkers." So Bob headed out to the Thunderbird location, where then-manager George Foreman assured him the main store was hiring people for the coming holiday season. He told Bob to go back and specifically ask for Frank Hanks.

Frank was skeptical. Bob was from the East Coast, a self-confessed ski bum who wore his hair long and had a beard and a mustache ("Dave always says you can't trust guys with mustaches," Frank says) and he kept waving around something Frank called a "reh-ZOOM-ee." He said he'd hire Bob, but only if he gave a year commitment.

"Frank said, 'We know what you people are like. You come out here, you get some money, then you take off to be a ski bum,'" Bob recalls. "He was right, but how did he know that?"

Frank gave the kid all of two minutes to consider the offer, and Bob accepted, promising to give him at least a year. "Frank pretty much threatened me that if I left within a year he was going to kick my ass," Bob says, still sporting facial hair and shoulder-length locks, 35 years later.

Ironically, Frank assigned Bob to the plumbing department — the one place in his grandfather's store he had avoided, because that's where Bob's father worked, and they didn't get along. Didn't matter. That's where Frank needed him and that's where he started as a salesman. Two and a half years later, Bob was promoted to plumbing department manager.

Bob was just another hard-working employee during the day, but he liked to stay late to get things done (don't bother calling federal wage authorities; as a manager, he didn't qualify for overtime), and once everybody else was gone, he liked to throw open the cage and let his inner ski bum/rock-and-roller run wild. He'd kick off his shoes and socks, crank up KBCO on the boom box, get himself fixed up with a bag of peanut M&Ms and a bottle of Pepsi and dance his way up and down the aisles, singing out loud. One time he was surprised when Dave and Dee stopped by after hours.

"Dee was horrified, 'What is that guy doing in our store?' Dave says, 'Oh, that's just Bob. He's doing orders,'" Bob recalls.

Bob couldn't believe such a large business could still maintain such a family atmosphere. McGuckin's was closed on every major holiday — and still is — so employees could enjoy time with their friends and family, and every year in December threw a sumptuous Christmas bash. Around 2000, when Dave decided everyone would probably rather have a bonus than attend a one-off $10,000 shindig, Bob started throwing his own party at Boulder Dark Horse Saloon for Christmas, inviting all past and present McGuckin's employees and featuring a house rock band. Now employees have a bonus and a party.

"I have never seen this many people who work or worked together drink and consume as much alcohol as we do and still get along," Bob says. "People from 1980 still show up at the party."

Moving into the big new store also marked the beginning of another celebrated McGuckin's tradition: Allowing customers to bring their dogs into the store when they shop, though it would soon evolve from "allowing" into "embracing." It all started when Dave started bringing his little terrier to keep him company in his upstairs office. Soon enough, she was tagging along every time he went down to the floor.

"People would come up and say, 'I just saw that guy has a dog — can we bring our dog in, too?'" Doc Dilkes says. "I don't know why most businesses don't allow it, but we said sure. Dave brings Maggie, so why not?"

The policy was controversial at first, and some customers complained. But Dave and Dee liked the idea; in dog-friendly Boulder, it was just one more way McGuckin's fit into the community. In the 35 years since, thousands of canines have walked in Maggie's pawsteps, and Doc can remember only a handful of unfortunate incidents, none serious. On balance, the dog-friendly policy has generated a wealth of goodwill for the store.

"I love taking the dogs to McGuckin's," says Boulder's Karen Eifler. "They get so much love there!"

Boulder's Nancy Wrigglesworth recently took her son's new puppy into the store to buy the dog a toy. "What I didn't expect were pup-level buckets full of toys," she says with amusement. "He stuck his nose in, sorted through it and chose his favorite. Of course McGuckin's made a sale!"

Today, there are water bowls placed strategically around the store, employees on the floor keep their green-vest pockets stocked with treats (and loaner leashes, so nobody's friend has to stay in the car) and are encouraged to greet canine visitors; many customers make a point to stop and greet dogs they pass in the aisles.

"My current dog was afraid of men when I first adopted him," says Tracey Berry, who started bringing her pet into the store for socialization training. "My idea of 'McGuckin Therapy' has and continues to nourish his curiosity and love of people."

But here's all you really need to know about how popular McGuckin's dog-friendly policy is: When a certain Atlanta-based home-improvement business came to town in 2006, so many customers complained that local managers had to request a waiver from corporate rules forbidding pets in the aisles. As Inc. magazine notes, "Home Depot was the one that had to adapt, imitating McGuckin's dog-friendly policy in this canine-crazy town."[57]

CHAPTER TEN

Hardware People

Finding nuts and bolts might be cause for alarm in the Soviet Union, but in Boulder, it's all in a day's work.

— 1989 Daily Camera story about McGuckin's salvaging a Russian student group's lost science project

By 1980, almost every vestige of Boulder's conservative, old-fashioned roots had been swept away by incoming tides of out-of-state residents and a whole new culture that would characterize it for the next four decades — liberal, outdoorsy, fit, hip, and wealthy.

The shift didn't agree with everyone.

"Boulder is full of rude, empty-headed, pushy fat cats and their offspring, and the nice people are being gradually pushed out or phased out," one old-time resident groused to the Daily Camera the day before the Pearl Street Mall dedication in 1977.[58]

Until 1972, Boulder's athletic reputation rested largely on the performance of CU's football team. The Buffaloes couldn't be called a perennial power, but rose up every few years to conquer some of college football's mightiest titans, defeating the Penn State Nittany Lions in 1970 and the LSU Tigers and Ohio State Buckeyes the following season, when the team lost only to Big Eight rivals Oklahoma and Nebraska and finished No. 3 in the nation behind those two powerhouses. The basketball team at CU also showed up here and there, winning the once-dominant NIT tournament and following late superstar Cliff Meely into the NCAA tourney in the late 1960s.

But in 1972, Boulder's sporting profile changed forever, when Frank Shorter took the gold medal in the marathon at the Munich Olympics — the first American to do so since 1908 — and the silver in the '76 Olympics in

Montreal. Shorter had excelled as a college athlete at Yale, winning the national cross country championships four years straight from 1970-1973. Shorter had plenty of inborn talent, but he also had a secret weapon: Training at high altitude in Boulder.

On Memorial Day 1979 Shorter and Boulder banker Steve Bosley launched the Bolder Boulder 10K race, and the city has never looked back, with more than 50,000 people running each year. CU's cross country teams have since won multiple national championships, and university and city runners have charged to the top of the rankings in countless events, from the 10K to ultramarathons (any race longer than 26.2 miles).

McGuckin's has never tried to co-opt the running boom, deferring to specialty stores such as Boulder Running Co., started by former world-champion marathoner Mark Plaatjes and Johnny Halberstadt. But it has played its part here and there. For example, hard-core runners who insist on going out no matter the weather — local runner Mike Sandrock boasts a "streak" of daily running extending back nearly two decades — have long turned to the store for a simple, low-tech method of improving their traction on snow and ice. All they have to do is walk in, head to the nuts-and-bolts aisle and tell whoever is working, "I'm a runner..." and they'll be politely interrupted and pointed to the box containing #6 hex-head, ¼-inch metal screws, which can be easily inserted into soles and provide outstanding traction, especially on ice.

But just about everyone agrees that McGuckin's was joined at the hip with the quirky Boulder Kinetic Sculpture Challenge — aka Kinetics — which was launched as a grassroots display of engineering prowess and creativity in 1980 and later vaulted to prominence when it won sponsorship from Boulder's hip, home-grown rock radio station KBCO. Kinetic-sculpture races are organized competitions between human-powered amphibious vehicles that began in Ferndale, California, in 1969 and were a natural for Boulder, home to hippies, engineers and partiers in equal numbers.

"That is a good question," answers the website for the organization descended from that first Boulder race when pondering why anyone would do such a thing. "There isn't any real need for kinetics beyond a bunch of people who want, for just one day out of the year ... to show off the contraptions they spent a moderate amount of time and effort and countless trips to (the hardware store) for that, in their mind, is the perfect solution to the kinetics equation."[59]

Bottom line? People spent countless hours building contraptions that they had to propel on land and sea — OK, Boulder Reservoir — while typically drinking a fair amount of beer and dressing up as cartoon characters, sharks, wizards, Wonder Woman … or whatever. And in Boulder, circa 1980, McGuckin Hardware was *the* place to go shopping for components.

"McGuckin's has always played a huge role in Kinetics. The event always benefited from the incredible diversity of McGuckin's inventory," says Ed Pomponi, who photographed that first race, has entered a craft every year since 1982 and now serves on the committee for the event, which moved to Longmont's Union Reservoir in 2010. "We would never have had our craft if not for that store."

Pomponi's 21st-century team still uses that first, 33-year-old craft, a feat made possible only because they can replace broken or lost parts at McGuckin's.

"McGuckin's has this old-time way of doing business," he says. "You can't go into Home Depot and, say, buy two nuts and two washers, and they don't have a selection of our old metric stock. … I'd say most of the teams from the Boulder area over the years, and a lot from out of state — everyone I know, for sure — goes to McGuckin's for the diversity of the product line and that way of doing business."

Unsurprisingly, teams came to McGuckin's, hat in hand, asking for sponsorship from that very first year. But staff members got to thinking about it and couldn't come up with a good reason not to just build their own craft. They were experts, after all, and they had access to more than 100,000 items with which to build the perfect Kinetic vehicle.

"We're hardware people! Let's just do our own," Doc Dilkes says.

Doc was a newbie and didn't join the team, but those who did took the effort very seriously. Brian Athearn, Kenny Phillips, Glen Mason and Robb Hight all spent countless hours working on the craft at Frank Hanks' house out by Boulder Reservoir — and being paid for it.

"I was stupid the first year," Dee says. "They all said, 'We're working overtime!' but they'd spend half the night drinking beer. The whole crew would just leave on Saturday and Sunday to work on that stupid kinetic thing. They wouldn't come to work!"

But in the end, the effort paid off … in a $100 gift certificate to Boulder's only strip club, the Bustop, the booby prize for coming in *dead last*. The team geared up to enter the next year, but never got a shot to repeat the ignominy.

"By the second year I said, 'You guys, I'm tired of us all working our butts off, and you're out here drinking beer and playing like little kids,'" says Dee, who laughs now, but confesses she was hopping mad at the time.

Another event that began at the same time not only stuck, but grew into one of the store's best-loved traditions, the Tent Sale. It started in 1979, with a couple of folding tables under a single pop-up tent, as a way to sell off discontinued merchandise, samples and slightly damaged goods.

"It was basically a yard sale. We got rid of a lot of junk, then just folded it up at night and carried it all back into the store," Doc says. "It worked that way for several years."

But the event attracted people in search of good deals, and store buyers began poking their sales reps and distributors for discontinued, recalled or reconditioned items to sell at bargain prices. The tent grew, and so did the sale, and soon McGuckin's was offering it in both fall and spring, a community event featuring both petting zoos and smashing deals. It's now marked in red on many Boulderites' calendars.

"It was very festive," Doc says. "It still is."

By the time the 1980s rolled around, it was becoming apparent that McGuckin's needed a technology upgrade. Dave had never been big on the idea of computerizing, believing that the store's enduring manual system put employees in a better position to get to know customers and familiarize themselves with the inventory. Perusing printed catalogs from suppliers and manufacturers, some nearly a foot thick, gave employees an excellent continuing education program in hardware.

"We knew those catalogs; we went through them all the time," Frank Hanks says.

Also, the store's on-the-spot ordering system, the "want card," seemed to be working just fine. All floor staff carried the cards — emblazoned with the McGuckin logo and cut with rounded corners so they would slip more easily in and out of a green vest pocket — and would fill one out whenever a customer requested an item. Those cards were transferred to a "want book"— a simple, spiral notebook that lived in the buyer's office. When John Haskovec started in 1975, the buyer was Ed Regal Sr., who occupied the only office in the store. Ed's desk sat in front of a poster of a mafia don in a pinstripe suit and black fedora, saying, "When I want your opinion, I'll ask you."

"He had an absolutely phenomenal memory of how to get any item, where to get it, who had the best prices, who was or wasn't shipping," recalls John, now a buyer for builders hardware in the store. "He'd proceed to get whatever you transcribed into the want book. You'd go back and forth about how many to order, but Ed learned from Dave that this way we'd get what the customers want, rather than a planogram"— a diagram of where and what products should be placed on retail shelves — "to meet some manufacturer's needs."

In the 21st century, almost all McGuckin's employees have upgraded to a higher-tech "want card" in the form of a smartphone. But not everyone.

"This is Bob's computer and cellphone right here," says store manager Bob Perkins, whipping a stack of want cards out of his vest pocket, "same as when I started working here in 1980. I absolutely still use the cards." Bob takes pride that he doesn't own a cellphone, only has a computer at his house because of work demands, "and I drive a '77 Toyota Land Cruiser and 'new' '95 4Runner."

Right up until the early '80s, Dave refused to install computerized cash registers. He preferred mechanical registers that he and his employees could service themselves, and again, he felt that a manual process was a learning tool for employees. But finally, even the service staff from National Cash Registers couldn't find parts to keep the old machines up and running, and McGuckin's bought computerized registers. They presented their own problems, including occasional loss of data during power outages or surges. Countless employees still recall when Don Glinsky, a computer service representative for NCR, decided to have a little fun with employees' lack of knowledge about computers. Glinsky had a little crush on a cashier named Lynn Mann, and one day he approached her with a deadly earnest expression and asked her a question that would no doubt earn him a trip to the HR department in these more sensitive times.

"You know," he began, "I'm kind of embarrassed to ask you this, but you have to understand static electricity can cause these machines to go haywire, so, do you happen to be wearing nylon underwear? Because that can screw things up."

Don took the joke further, advising Frank that he should instruct his cashiers not to wear fancy underwear. At least that was better than when Dee told Frank around the same time that he needed to tell his cashiers to wear bras because customers were leering during checkout.

But Lynn Mann didn't seem to mind the remark, given that she married Glinsky not long after.

Though it was hardly in his plans, Dave Hight found himself in charge of a non-hardware venture in 1981. In 1976, CU business professor John Hess had gotten the idea to build a health club in Boulder, which was fast becoming a fitness mecca. Hess put together a group of investors, including such local luminaries as former CU football players Phil Irwin and Bobby Anderson — who spent five seasons playing for the NFL's Denver Broncos, New England Patriots and Washington Redskins —to open Rally Sport Health and Fitness Club (the "rally" referred to racquetball, an immensely popular recreational sport at the time) at 2727 29th St., which happened to be a property owned by Dave Hight and two other men.

But by 1981, the club was circling the drain. Rather than let Hess take the company into bankruptcy, Dave Hight decided to buy him out and reorganize, to protect his own investment, since he owned shares in the company and had loaned Hess money to keep it going. After a false start with a new manager, Dave turned in 1983 to Dennis DiPaula, who had been a janitor at the club, once more trusting his gut over a resume to find the right man.

"Let's just say teaching business as a theory and doing it are two different things; the business was not in great shape when I took over," DiPaula says. "Dave told me, 'If you can turn this thing around, you'll own it someday.' I didn't put much stock in that."

The years went by, and DiPaula indeed resurrected the club, which is still going strong today. In the 1990s, after he'd gotten married, he got a job offer to run a bigger club in San Francisco. But just in case Dave had been serious all those years ago, Denny went to ask if the offer had been for real.

"Dave said, 'I told you years ago, when the time is right, I'll turn it over to you, let you buy me out,'" Denny recalls. On a hunch, he turned down the California job and stayed at Rally. "Then one day about a year later he turned up out of nowhere and said, 'I want to take you down to Denver tomorrow.'"

Dave drove down to Denver with DiPaula, who was still in the dark about what was going on. They took the elevator to a well-appointed office with spectacular views of the Rockies on the top floor of the "cash register" building at 1740 Broadway in downtown Denver. There, Dave told his attorney he was turning the fitness business over to DiPaula, and laid out in precise detail how it was going to happen.

"Driving back to Boulder I'm just staring out the window. My whole life had just changed. It was a big deal. I'd spent a lot of years turning that place around. Dave said, 'How does it feel?' 'It feels good, Dave. I'm still coming to grips with it,'" DiPaula says.

But Dave kept pressing for a more detailed response. Finally he phrased the question this way: "How does it feel to be a millionaire?"

"I said, 'I don't have two cents to rub together!' He nodded and said, 'That's how it feels,'" DiPaula says, laughing. "It's just such a great story. ... He's such a man of integrity. Who do you know who would do something like that on a handshake from 15 years before? I always thought one of his sons would come in and take over" — Robb Hight had even helped manage the club for a time — "and there were plenty of people who would have bought the club. This just goes to his character."

Business continually expanded at the new store, but the Thunderbird satellite hadn't come along for the ride. Cowboy Slick Spaur ran the place from 1965 to 1973, but no matter who was managing, whether it was good old reliable Ran Ransom or Jimmy Marsh (who really just wanted to be a minister), it never did more than limp along.

Dave recalls the time a woman popped in and asked if she could borrow a fertilizer spreader, a courtesy the Thunderbird store extended to customers. But when he took it out to her car he saw she had a trunkful of Scott's fertilizers; same stuff he sold at the store, but she'd bought it next door at Safeway.

"It was one of my best-selling things. (But) the old guy from Scott's died, IT&T took it over, and they no longer honored a dealership," Dave says. He wasn't even aware that the behemoth grocery store was selling the same products he stocked, but at cost. McGuckin's wasn't allowed to cut its prices, per the dealer, but Dave wasn't about to stand around twiddling his thumbs while some corporate chain did its best to undersell him. He called the Scott's rep and told him to come take all his stuff out of the store.

Then one day in 1986, Dave stood by while a Thunderbird cashier spent about a half-hour walking around the small store with a customer, showing him the parts he needed to repair a sink, including ⅜th-inch compression fittings, the kind of thing McGuckin's kept on hand when everyone else had to order it. At the register, the customer let on that he'd bought some of the supplies he needed at Hugh M. Woods, a hardware and lumber outlet owned by national chain Payless Cashways that had opened in Gunbarrel several years earlier. The guy allowed that he would have bought that stuff from McGuckin's, too, but it was "too expensive."

"I asked why he bought the rest of it at our store," Dave recalls, "and the guy said, 'Well, (Hugh M. Woods) didn't have any of that, any of the little stuff.'"

As soon as the customer left, Dave instructed the employee to go get the CLOSED sign from the back. "I'd been trying to figure out what to do with this store, and that guy just made up my mind. Every time I'm out in this rich neighborhood people work you over about price. It was Friday, and I put the sign up and said, 'You guys take the weekend off.'"

Monday morning, Dave and Frank hauled everything from Thunderbird to the main store, and that was that. "We were out there 21 years," Dave says with a shrug, "and we never made a nickel out of it."

Although McGuckin's first experiment with a co-op had ended unceremoniously with Dave offering unconventional proctology advice to a representative from Chicago-based Ace Hardware, by the mid-1980s joining a co-op made good business sense.

Dave, in particular, was no fan of the co-op system, which by then had begun to overwhelm the network of family-owned "jobbers" he'd been working with since he was just a kid at Leffingwell's in Brighton. Townley Metal and Hardware out of Kansas City, established in 1884, Nebraska-based Dutton Lainson (1886), Holmes Hardware of Pueblo (1891) and other long-time family jobbers were being driven out of business.

"I always felt that the co-op system had put my family wholesalers out of business, not through competition, but loopholes in the tax code" that exempted companies from one layer of income tax that family-held concerns still had to pay, Dave says. "I always liked doing business with a family concern; they were in the same boat I was in. Townley's financed me when the banks wouldn't loan me any money."

But co-ops gave members access to huge regional distribution centers and allowed them take advantage of volume pricing. With all McGuckin's serious competitors belonging to vast national chains, it didn't merely make sense to band together with thousands of other independent retailers; it would have been suicide not to.

"It gives you central buying and distribution centers, and banding together gives greater marketing value. It gives you some leverage," says Barry Hight, now president of McGuckin's. "In 1986, we were just paying too much for too many things."

McGuckin's had been courted by various co-ops for years, including California-based Hometown Hardware and remarkably, Ace Hardware, thanks to a former Townley's salesman who contacted Dave after he started working for the co-op. Dave was willing to let bygones be bygones, but he drew the line at Ace's demand that he put the company's name on the front of his store; ditto for Hometown Hardware.

But there was one co-op that Dave thought he could work with. True Value hadn't had a partner in Boulder since Valentine's shut down in 1972, but by 1986 had some 3,000 independent members and a dozen regional distribution centers. The co-op was established in Chicago in 1948 by John Cotter as Cotter & Company, with 12 members. Today the co-op has some 6,000 members but it's still owned by the Cotter family.[60]

"They don't tell us what to do," Barry says. "These others require you to put their name on the door, but with True Value you don't have to do that."

"And I wouldn't have taken them on if I'd had to," Dave says. "They are family-owned, which I like. We still buy from 3,000 sources, but we are one of the 15 largest accounts for True Value. They've got quite a few independent stores in Colorado, so we end up helping out those stores, too."

From time to time, McGuckin's employees hear from customers who "heard you sold out to a big corporation" and they have to explain how the True Value co-op works. And membership, as they say, has its privileges — for customers, too — as a certain catastrophically rainy week in September 2013 demonstrated. Having the True Value warehouse in Denver gave McGuckin's access to hundreds of sump pumps, box fans and more within hours.

"It's great to have that warehouse in Denver," Dave says, noting that he had a hunch and sent a truck down U.S. 36 to pick up 100 stock sump-pumps just weeks before seven soggy days in May 2015 caused flooding and pushed demand through the roof.

By the end of the 1980s, Boulder's population had grown to more than 83,000 — three times more than when Bill McGuckin opened his doors in 1955. McGuckin employed 150 people, 100 of them fulltime, and now offered some 300,000 items. But the store's influence can't be stated in mere numbers. It had become an icon. As a Denver Post columnist enthused, "It's the kind of place you go for a hardware 'fix.' Here no one will think you're odd if you spend an hour or two just looking around."[61]

McGuckin's was gaining a reputation beyond Boulder, beyond Colorado, even beyond the United States.

"Finding nuts and bolts might be cause for alarm in the Soviet Union, but in Boulder, it's all in a day's work," proclaimed a 1989 Daily Camera story about a team of Soviet youth who had lost their entry to the Odyssey of the Mind competition somewhere between Moscow and Boulder. "We'll never find what we need," moaned one of the students. But that, as the Camera writer noted, "was before they were introduced to McGuckin Hardware."[62]

CHAPTER ELEVEN

Bad Dog Next Door

It's the crème de la crème, period.

— A competitor on McGuckin Hardware

Despite the constant arrival of new challengers, McGuckin Hardware entered the 1990s wearing the buckle as Boulder's undisputed hardware champion. As a privately owned company, the store doesn't release its sales or revenue figures to the public, but in 1980, Hardware Merchandising magazine estimated sales at $6 million. And business had only grown. Dave Hight estimates that McGuckin's sales quadrupled during the time it moved from the original locations to the larger store, from 1973 to 1978.

"And since then we probably do about seven times as much business," he says.

In 1992 a small expansion brought the store from 36,000 square feet to 42,000 square feet, and employee numbers had climbed from 100 to 150 (45 part time).[63] That year the store opened its power and equipment service center, and in 1993 it added another 20,000 square feet, bringing the total to more than 60,000 square feet, as part of an overall $1.4 million revamping of the Village Shopping Center, by then owned by the Honolulu-based estate of James Campbell.[64] The facelift added new sales-floor space, offices upstairs and a new entrance from Canyon Boulevard.

Marketing and sales director Roger Wood insisted that the expansion "wasn't motivated by a desire to fend off the threat of a new rival, such as Builders Square or HomeBase," according to a Daily Camera business story. However, Vicky Gits reported, "rumors of such a warehouse-style, home-hardware store locating in Boulder have been circulating for several months."[65]

Whatever the reason, customers and journalists continued to talk about

McGuckin's in breathless superlatives.

According to a 1995 Denver Post roundup of the Denver metro area's best hardware stores, "You can get anything you want at McGuckin's (sic) Hardware in Boulder, which is legendary for its exhaustive inventory and attentive service. A hardware addict's dream store. 'It's the crème de la crème, period,' said one competitor."[66]

In the midst of such growth and success, the Hights were constantly hearing from people who wanted them to start franchising and corporations that wanted to buy them out. But the Thunderbird experience had soured Dave on the idea of expansion. He loved simply going to work at the main location, and any time someone tried to entice him into moving into other cities or franchising, he said he preferred that other families start their own businesses, and he'd offer them everything he knows for free. One company offered $4 million for the family to walk away. When Dave asked what they would do with the store, he was told they planned to sell the inventory and shut it down.

"At the time I had 150 employees," he says. "They would have all lost their jobs."

Still, this was the go-go '90s, and around the time of the remodel the family decided to bring in a business consultant who convinced them that the time to "modernize" had come. The family needed to devise a formal "succession plan," and the first step was to get all family members off the payroll. They would be shareholders and serve on the board, but basically, they were told it was time to scram. It seemed to make sense; at least, that's what the rest of the business world — or at least the suit-and-tie-wearing types — was always talking about.

Brent, Barry and Robb left their jobs (technically, at any rate) and in theory Dave was out of the loop on any kind of management decisions. Robb, gregarious and fun, had always excelled at working with customers but now headed off to Hood River, Oregon, where he windsurfed and built a house for his wife and two daughters. Oldest son Brent, who had overseen McGuckin's Penguin Wheel business in the 1970s and managed its small-engine repair and service, moved to Kona, Hawaii, where he managed a coffee plantation for three years before returning to Colorado, where he took a job with the Sil-Terhar auto dealership.

Barry had become an excellent mechanic when he was younger, specializing in German cars — Porsches, Volkswagens, Audis —and showed an aptitude for management while working at the store. Although they'd been "fired," as they put it, both he and his father somehow managed to not quite leave the store when they were supposed to. That little bit of stubbornness may have saved McGuckin's.

On the advice of the consultant, the company brought in an outsider, Jim Paddock, to manage the store during the transition, signing him to a three-year contract in 1992. The new manager's agenda included creating an employee manual, formal job descriptions and implementing formal employee reviews, all things that probably needed to be done at a business that had resisted using a time clock until the late 1970s. But groomed in a corporate environment, Paddock simply was not a good fit for the culture. He often used a corporate argot both baffling and pretentious to people like Frank Hanks, Ran Ransom and Bob Perkins. They were no longer "employees," but rather "teammates" or "associates" and for some reason they were was supposed to be "buying into" nebulous concepts like "synergy" and "paradigm shifts" while "staying in their swim lanes" and "empowering" themselves to … something or other.

And there were meetings. Lots and lots of meetings. But not enjoyable meetings. Not the kind where everybody worked late on Friday and pitched in a couple of bucks for beer and snacks, or the famous "centipede" meetings during which everyone sat on the conveyor belt in the back kicking around ideas, legs dangling down.

"We just went very corporate," Barry says.

"He wanted more of a cookie-cutter approach," Dave says.

Paddock took the job description process so seriously that he insisted on putting different types of employees in vests of different colors, denoting different responsibilities. Green for sales, navy blue for stockers, gold for managers, royal blue for cashiers. The idea was to help customers know who to approach with questions.

But a funny thing happened in the transition from Irish green to the new manager's rainbow. Instead of learning the old McGuckin Way — everyone helps out in whatever way necessary to serve the customers and the business — some new employees assumed a "That's not my job" attitude. Barry remembers asking a new sales staff member to help him stock some items in the sports department. "Nope," the kid told him, "I was hired for sales."

"The different vests 'caste system' didn't work," Barry says. "I told (the new employee) that at McGuckin's everybody pitches in and told him to follow me back to housewares. There was Dad stocking garbage cans. I said, 'See that guy? Know what he does?' He said 'no,' and I told him that he was not only one of the store's best sales guys, but also the owner. 'And if it's good enough for the owner, it's good enough for you. But I don't expect somebody to do something I wouldn't do, either.' He didn't last long."

Had Paddock not been signed to a three-year contract, he surely wouldn't have, either. But this "new" McGuckin's was tearing the family, and the staff, apart. Frank Hanks, who had insisted on joining Dave to work nights and weekends back in 1968 and served as manager since 1969, up and quit.

"I loved working with Dave, but I had to tell him this just wasn't working for me," Frank says, shaking his head.

There is a chapter in "Dandelion Wine," Ray Bradbury's seminal novel of small-town life in 1928 Illinois, in which an out-of-town cousin sweeps into the Spaulding family's life, determined to "modernize" and set things right. She starts by reorganizing Grandma's kitchen, which had been a total mess, with mislabeled crocks and jars, misplaced implements, broken reading glasses and in general, chaos. The cousin even buys the half-blind old lady a cookbook.

"I don't need one of those," Grandma protests. "A handful of this, a pinch of that, a thimbleful of something else is all I ever use…"

Because Grandma's cooking had been so indescribably delicious before Aunt Rose's "reorg," the family members and boarders waited with watering mouths to see what she would create with the benefit of this new, organized, modern kitchen. This, Grandfather tells young Douglas, "is going to be a night in history." But constrained by someone else's idea of how she should do things, Grandma loses her magic, and the meal is terrible. The old woman retreats to her room, weeping.

Something similar was happening at good, old-fashioned McGuckin's, the family business that had made so many people so happy for so many years. After Frank left, Dave didn't enjoy his own business any more. He was feeling depressed, Barry says, and his old support system was falling apart.

"I called the family counselor who had recommended it all and told him, 'I can't watch this. This hurts,'" Barry says. He recognized that much of what Paddock was trying to do *was* important and that a company the size of McGuckin's couldn't go on forever without making some of the changes he was trying to effect. But Barry also knew there was a balance to be struck, and Paddock's corporate management style wasn't working for either the family or its loyal, long-time employees.

"He just didn't put the same emphasis as Dave on the well-being of the employees. In fact, a lot of the employees really didn't like him or his management style. And we'd always been loyal to our suppliers, but he was coming at it with more of a corporate, bottom-line attitude," Barry says.

"The question became, 'How do I streamline the business to take advantage of technology, keeping it on track, but keep people happy and doing their jobs well, having pride in what they do?'" Barry says. "You want to move and be successful and not go out of business, but too often companies seem to take people out of the equation."

In Bradbury's small-town fable, upon pondering endless "sad breakfasts, melancholy lunches and funereal dinners," 12-year-old Douglas steals into the kitchen that night of the disastrous dinner and throws everything back into the disarray that made his grandmother a culinary enchantress who set mouths watering three times a day, every day.[67] When they coax the old woman back to the kitchen, and Grandfather places her old, cracked glasses on her nose, the next meal is more heavenly than ever, leaving readers to ponder the moral to the story.

Barry didn't vandalize McGuckin's. Instead, he went back to the consultant to tell him what the changes were doing to his father, the family, the employees. He was going to resume a management job at the store, where he'd be happy to work under Paddock while schooling him subtly in the McGuckin Way. And if the new manager wasn't creative or flexible enough to both modernize and keep what was best about the business, well, he'd be out of there.

"Barry," Dave says simply, "got really mad about what was happening."

But try as he might, Barry's subtle guerrilla efforts failed to "McGuckinize" Paddock. Barry sat agitatedly through meeting after pointless meeting, wondering why everything seemed to require six months of "planning" and "strategy" before anyone was allowed to take action. He found the new regime too slow, too unresponsive, too deaf to the concerns of employees.

"I knew the car was broken. But my dad raised me to think, 'If it's broke, then let's fix it,'" Barry says.

Paddock would not, in the end, graduate from "McGuckin University." His contract was not renewed in 1995, and the store's brief fling with impersonal corporate culture was decidedly over. The business reorganized, upgraded its procedures and technology, carrying many of Paddock's best ideas to completion. Barry was named president, Dave CEO and Dee secretary/treasurer, while Brent and Robb remained as shareholders and owners of the business they, too, had helped build.

"All three of Dave and Dee's boys could be found in the stores on Arapahoe through the '70s and '80s, learning the business and working side by side with the store associates," says their childhood contemporary, Terry Gallagher. "They were all there when the new store was constructed, and they were instrumental in helping their father and a great staff take (McGuckin's) to the next level."

If Barry hadn't come in to take charge, Dave says he'd have packed it in.

"If we didn't have family in this business, I would probably just close it out. The only way to run it is with family," Dave says. "We saw (with Paddock) that other people don't necessarily have the vision we have. It's taken us a lot of years to get here, and despite what everyone keeps saying, we can compete with the large stores and chains by running (McGuckin's) the same way Bill ran it when he was alive, and how I ran the company store up in Climax.

"My vision was always to fit into the community, to stock the things the handyman and carpenters and average homeowner needed immediately," he says.

Following Paddock's departure, Dave asked Frank Hanks to come back as COO, and in 1998 Joann became the office manager; both would stay until retiring in 2006.

"Dave is the type of person who was always just trying to make the place successful," Frank says. "People may look and think he's rich, but he never did take much pay. He took what he had to live on, and put everything else back into the store, into inventory, into his employees."

"Talking with Dad and Grandpa," says Barry's son Jason Hight, assistant store manager and a fourth-generation McGuckin family employee, "they have always done what works for the people, not what works for shareholders. We have a setting where the people who work for us are the *reason* it works, really, and we're not going to change that. We've never had to try to get rid of a bunch of people to make shareholders happy."

Sink or swim, it was the McGuckin's Way, or the highway.

The company emerged from its mid-'90s identity crisis more streamlined and modern, yet still infused with the charm and community-focused ethic that had served it so well for four decades. And once more Bill McGuckin's little hardware store was facing out-of-town corporate competition and predictions of doom. Though unmentioned in the Daily Camera's 1993 roster of potential corporate competitors, two giant chains set up shop near Boulder in 1996 and 1997.

Home Depot was a relative newcomer to the hardware business, opening its first two stores in Atlanta on June 22, 1979, each featuring 60,000 square feet—a size McGuckin's had taken nearly 40 years to grow into. The company is truly a "big box" store, literally boasting that its stores were "cavernous warehouses that dwarfed all competition" from the outset, realizing the founders' "vision of one-stop shopping for the do-it-yourselfer."[68] The company began selling shares on the NASDAQ exchange in 1981 and moved to the New York Stock Exchange in 1984, opening its 100th store in 1989. It crossed borders into Canada in 1994 with the purchase of the Aikenhead's chain of home-improvement centers. It "began flying its flag proudly in Mexico" in 2001 and would later expand into China, the United Kingdom and South America.

Eagle Hardware & Garden was, by comparison, a bit of a bantamweight, but still had plenty of punch. Founded in Renton, Washington, Eagle opened its first store in November 1990 but sported an astounding 100,000 square feet of space and a huge sign proclaiming, "More of everything!" The company went public in 1992, and in 1995 generated $615 million in sales at its 40 giant stores, mostly in the West, proclaiming itself the only hardware monolith capable of withstanding the Home Depot juggernaut: "This is war," founder David J. Heerensperger told Forbes magazine in 1996. "They are aiming for us, but we are a thorn in their side. Eagle is the first home-improvement center" — the now-familiar corporate name for "hardware store" — they haven't completely run over."[69]

By the time Home Depot opened a 100,000-square-foot store in Louisville — just 8 miles down U.S. 36 from McGuckin's — on Aug. 22, 1996, the corporation's annual revenues on 2,200 stores were $19.5 billion. Just across the way, Eagle opened a 135,000-square-foot outlet not even a quarter-mile away on Jan. 2, 1997. Home Depot officials crowed that, "Its location off U.S. 36 and McCaslin Boulevard was a faster drive for South Boulder residents than a trip to McGuckin."[70]

The Daily Camera uneasily editorialized on the sudden wealth of hardware options available to area residents, praising McGuckin's and 100-year-old, family-owned Steinbaugh Hardware in Louisville as well as the new corporate interlopers.

"Which of these stores will be standing five or 10 years from now?" The writer, then-Executive Editor Barrie Hartman, concluded, "We find ourselves agreeing with Home Depot's manager, John Brogan, when he says the defining factor for success and survival will be 'the store which gives the best customer service.'"[71]

Down at McGuckin's, everyone was ready for the competition. Managers estimated that the store's inventory overlapped with Home Depot by just 25 percent and swore they weren't worried. They did, however, find their new competitor's tactics distasteful, accusing the outlet of selling cheap knock-offs of top products, playing "bait and switch" with customers on pricing and, most irritating, loudly comparing their prices to those at the local independent in Boulder. But the company may not have fully understood how Boulder felt about McGuckin's.

"I remember when Home Depot opened in Louisville, everybody was worried. Their 'friend' McGuckin's was being threatened. It was like a bad dog had moved in next door," Bruce Ramp says. "People would come ask us, 'Are you guys going to be OK?' Then Home Depot, in its infinite wisdom, started putting price tags for McGuckin's right next to theirs. The sons of bitches were trying to put McGuckin's out of business. People came back to us and said that was bad karma, they were hitting below the belt. People strayed, but nine months later, they came back."

The perennial knock on McGuckin's is that its prices are too high, compared to corporate competitors. In some cases, that's true enough. But in the McGuckin's Way, price isn't everything, and if you want to support your community by paying your employees enough to raise a family and paying taxes that corporate stores avoid, then sure, sometimes you are going to pay a little more. But not always. In fact, not nearly as often as competitors would have customers believe.

"My day gets made all the time when a consumer comes in and says, 'Let me tell you something, Home Depot has got this at $4.29 and you guys are like $3.49.' … Or we'll get a good buy on a dozen table saws and they claim to match all our prices. I love getting those calls from Home Depot saying, 'How are you doing that?' I say, 'We just buy better than you do,'" Barry says. "My dad taught me a great ethics class just by growing up with him. When you put signs up with Hugh M. Woods' or McGuckin's prices, to me, that's not my kind of retailing. We'll stand on service, stand on knowing our customers."

Measuring customer service is a notoriously inexact, anecdotal pursuit, but one in which McGuckin's has always come out ahead. And despite the confidence of the Louisville Home Depot manager in 1996, Boulder's beloved independent was winning the customer-service battle by the numbers, at least: Home Depot had 80 employees to cover its 135,000-square-foot store and Eagle employed the same number to cover 140,000 square feet, compared to the 150 experts who roamed the aisles at McGuckin's 60,000-square-foot store. Walk into McGuckin's and a customer had four times as many people to help him than at the big-box stores.

"It's not just, 'Hello, how are you?' either," Jason Hight says. "When you want to talk to an expert in any department, we have one on the floor at just about all times."

McGuckin's hadn't fought the final round with its big orange competitor from Atlanta, but everyone took satisfaction in learning that the Louisville outlet was one of the chain's more underperforming stores, according to Barry.

Meanwhile, Louisville's Eagle outlet was swallowed up in the company's 1999 corporate takeover by another heavyweight that would still be punching away like a Rock 'em Sock 'em Robot at Home Depot in 2015, Lowe's.

The year Home Depot opened nearby, McGuckin's was busy breaking its all-time sales record and opening the McGuckin Design Center, a kitchen and bath hardware and fixtures outlet, across the parking lot on the site of Annie Joratz's motel. Barry told a reporter that 1997 "is going to be another good year — a great year, in fact."[72]

But Steinbaugh Hardware, started as a blacksmith shop in 1892 by J.J. Steinbaugh, provided a cautionary tale. The store was unable to withstand the proximity of two big corporate retailers and closed its doors for good in 1997.

CHAPTER TWELVE

'Try It! It's Boulder!'

You mean the *best hardware store in the universe?*
— Adventure athlete and author Aron Ralston,
asked to describe McGuckin's

Bernadette Tillis is a newbie by McGuckin's standards, with "just" 24 years under her belt. Originally from Los Angeles, she played basketball at Colorado State University from 1989-1991 and fell in love with Boulder when the team came down to play CU. After graduation she could think of no better place to look for a summer job.

"I applied at two places," says Bernadette, who with Bob Perkins serves as store manager. "I guess I was meant to work for the Hight family, though I didn't know it — I applied at just two places, McGuckin's and RallySport."

She got offers from both businesses, but not for the positions she'd applied for. Rather than work in food service at the health club, she took a job as a cashier at McGuckin's. She figured she'd just stay for the summer, but found she loved working at the store. Both her parents had owned businesses while she was growing up, and she could see that this place was very family-oriented.

"I sure didn't think I'd be here long," she says. "But Barry was just so welcoming to me, even as a new hire. How many places in the corporate world does the company president know your name in the first month?"

Bernadette's green-vested career mirrors those of other long-time employees, including Ran Ransom, Frank and Joann Hanks, Earl Duncan, Bob Perkins, John and Marsha Haskovec, Bruce Ramp and others: She started small, worked hard, demonstrated a willingness to learn and was soon on her way up the ladder.

"Dave says he can tell in two days if someone is going to have what it takes to work here. Does this person keep busy and work well with other people? Are they trying to avoid work, or do they jump in?" says manager Doc Dilkes. "It takes me a couple of weeks, but you know if someone is going to work out."

Bernadette asked then-department manager Larry Metzger what was the fastest way to move up in the company, and he advised her to get on the sales floor. Seven months in she took a sales job in the botanical department, then gradually took positions in other categories, going on to manage five departments. She also single-handedly took McGuckin's small pet-products section and created today's full-scale pet food and supplies department.

"That happens to be one of the categories that's done extremely well," Doc says. "Ten years ago, nobody would buy a $75 bag of dog food, but today they do. People in Boulder want the best for their dogs."

Boulderites also love their holidays, and since Bruce Ramp slapped together that first Christmas display in 1976, McGuckin's has come to be known as one of the best places in town to shop for holiday items and décor. Once Bruce realized that the store's distribution partners didn't offer a very big selection of Christmas and other holiday items, he took to the road for the next 28 years, attending shows around the country in search of stuffed Santas, unique European ornaments and even gag items, like the three $700 upside-down Christmas trees he read about in the Wall Street Journal.

"I traveled four or five times a year to New York, Dallas, Seattle, L.A. on my own, and I found stuff that people just don't see around here," Bruce says. He honed his expertise, huddling with rabbis to learn how to shop for menorahs, candles and other Jewish holiday items and queried the Sons of Norway about what Norwegian Christmas items they'd buy.

"To this day, people tell me that we are the best Hanukkah decoration store in the city," says McGuckin's marketing manager Louise Garrels.

"We went every year to McGuckin's to buy their hand-painted German Christmas ornaments," says Diane Rice of Boise, Idaho, who grew up in Boulder in the 1970s. "They were quite unique."

Bruce also realized from the moment he began holiday buying that most stores are myopic about the category. From stoned hippies in the 1970s to people planning weddings and golf tournaments to party-hearty CU students, everyone loves pretty colored lights, and not just in December.

"Ninety percent of those lights come from (Asia) ... shipped in August and September," Bruce says. "There is a complete drought the rest of the year except for stores with the smarts to hold on to the inventory for year-round sales. We do a really nice year-round business in Christmas lights."

But then, McGuckin's has always been willing to try new things.

"Lots of people come to us with inventions and products and we say, 'Give us a case of 'em and we'll try to sell them for a couple of months," Doc says, whether it's candy, cards, calendars or something more expensive.

For example, the store was the only authorized Boulder dealer of the Segway — the two-wheeled, self-balancing, battery-powered electric vehicle launched to great hype and fanfare in 2001 — for two years. ("We didn't sell any," Doc says with a shrug. "Luckily we didn't have to invest any money in them.") Mountain States Specialties, a family-owned Boulder company that distributes promotional products such as pins, patches, keychains, calendars and T-shirts, has been using McGuckin's as a proving ground for new wares for more than 35 years.

"If you come out with a product and submit it to corporate headquarters in California or Arkansas, you have to wait 16 months to get an answer," says Rich Lechman, part of the third generation to work for the family-owned and -operated company. "At McGuckin's you send a buyer over to show them, and you might have a thumbs-up in a day. By the time the big-box store gives approval the item might not even be in vogue anymore."

McGuckin's might be old-fashioned in many ways, but its willingness to experiment has on occasion put hipness in its grasp. Trent Bush, a 1988 graduate of Boulder High School who started Twist Clothing Company, one of the nation's first snowboarding apparel companies, with his brother Troy and Boulder entrepreneurs Amani King, Justin Hostynek and Evan Hecox in 1989, remembers when the store was literally the only place in town to "buy a snowboard before it caught on. They may have been one of the first Burton accounts in Colorado, and therefore, the world."

Having heard of McGuckin's willingness to try new products, Seattle-based Cascade Designs had a hunch that its Therm-a-Rest air mattresses — tough nylon pads with an inflatable, polyurethane core that is now standard-issue equipment for outdoor enthusiasts seeking to soften the impact of gnarly tree roots and the warmth-sucking vampire of cold dirt—would sell in Boulder.

"I saw it at a show in Chicago and I said, 'I love it. This product is excellent. I think I might have a hard time selling it at $40 when people can pay $6 for a roll of insulation, but let's try anyway,'" Doc says. "Experiment. Be bold. Try it. It's Boulder, just try it. No matter how exotic or expensive, just try it."

By the dawn of the 21st century McGuckin's had evolved into something much more than a retail outlet, even an iconic one. Its countless fans made it, literally, a tourist attraction, a place to settle fussy babies and occupy husbands, a form of therapy, a mother of invention, a management school, a training ground, a doggy playground, a final resting place, a wedding chapel, celebrity sighting spot, a rehab and more.

"Women come from out of town all the time to buy at my store," says Elfriede Gamow, whose store just across Canyon Boulevard, Elfriede's Fine Fabrics, has sold fabric, buttons, trim, lace and other hard-to-find embellishments for heirloom sewing projects since 1974. "We send the men over to McGuckin's, and if anything, they stay longer."

"We go to McGuckin's almost every weekend," says Boulder native Joan McLean Braun, a 1977 graduate of Boulder High School. "My usual response to the 'Can I help you?' inquiry is, 'Do you know where my husband went? I know he's in here somewhere.'"

Tracey Berry, who moved to Boulder in 1978, says hanging out at McGuckin's is cheaper and more effective than paying for a shrink, a nanny or doggy daycare.

"Whenever I want to block out how much Boulder has changed, I grab a coffee at the Brewing Market and walk around the aisles of McGuckin's. I love the way it smells, how friendly everyone is who wears the green vest and how it can ... transport me back in time to 1978 when I first came to Boulder. It ... reminds me of old friends and old times. I call it 'McGuckin Therapy,'" Berry says. "It's also where I take my dogs for a good time."

When Karen Breunig Hine's 6-month-old daughter was colicky in the late 1980s, the only thing that would bring her solace was to put her in a cart and walk up and down the fan aisle at McGuckin's.

"It was magic, fans of all sizes and wind speeds. She would quiet right down. And the staff was so kind and understanding of this exhausted, bleary-eyed mom," she says.

Countless hundreds of local teenagers have gotten their first job experience wearing McGuckin green, and many were surprised to take home more than a paycheck every two weeks. Risa Johnson was just one of four young Fergusons who worked at the store during high school and college. Now a training specialist in human resources at Ball Aerospace & Technologies Corp. in Boulder, she still marvels at the way McGuckin's managers blended and balanced so many part-time student workers with the full-time staff and managers.

"Having a crew of capable high school and college employees enabled full-time and career employees to have traditional 8 to 5 schedules who could overlap with the part-time crew, yet never made the part-timers feel 'second best,'" she says.

Johnson, her siblings and other student workers quickly came to appreciate the store's willingness to arrange their schedules to accommodate school activities and treat everyone with the same level of respect. She'd worked jobs for two chain restaurants, and "There was no comparison in terms of how I was treated."

"To be honest, they completely spoiled me for how employers should treat their employees if they want them to be dedicated and fully engaged," she says. "I learned so much about life, employment, customer service, leadership, respect, employee engagement (and) hard work from my days at McGuckin's, things that have helped me in every job (and) role I've ever had. ... As a parent, I have found myself wishing there were other such employers today" for part-time student workers.

Mark Whitehouse, who as a boy brought the injured duck into the store for repair, has worked in human resources for more than 20 years and credits McGuckin's for teaching him how to treat employees of all kinds.

"As a little boy McGuckin Hardware was the first store I ever knew of (that) hired people with disabilities because of their great customer service and how they helped out the customers," he says. "They never seem to look at the disability or color or anything that seems to grab headlines today, (and) some of the solutions these employees came up with were remarkable. They actually laid the foundation of how I look at employees — what can they do, not what are their limitations."

Alana Linton, a switchboard operator for Boulder's famous Leanin' Tree publishing company — another longtime local business stalwart, founded by Ed Trumble in 1949 — and a 1985 graduate of Boulder High School, remembers how McGuckin's not only hired a relative with an addiction problem, but helped him.

"He was an alcoholic to the point that many other companies might have fired him, but they stood behind him and supported him in his sobriety process. I've always thought so well of McGuckin's (because of) that," she says. "Plus, if you can't find something in your house, check McGuckin's — they will probably have it."

McGuckin's has been so much a part of some people's lives that at least two (and almost certainly more) families wanted it to be the final resting place of their earthly remains. One woman scattered ashes of a loved one throughout the bins in the nuts and bolts aisle; employees found out about it only after she wrote a letter to the store. Then there was Henry Nelson Bull, inventor of the refrigerator magnet, who died Oct. 25, 1998, at age 92. When his son Jeff began looking into urns for his father's ashes, he found them not just too expensive, but too pretentious, too not-Henry. So he headed down to his father's favorite store in search of an appropriate receptacle.

"Sure enough, at McGuckin's there were some nice tin paint cans. I thought, 'Hmmm, Henry would be into the functionality of that,'" Jeff Bull told the weekly Boulder Planet. In the end, he and his girlfriend chose a nice Thermos bottle that was way more Henry than either a paint can or an expensive steel box. Alas, when they went outside to decant the pebbly gray ashes, Henry overflowed the Thermos bottle.

"So finally we moved to the bushes and ... well, we ended up leaving a couple of cups of Henry spread out around McGuckin Hardware. That was great. He loved McGuckin's," his son said. It was strictly a bonus that Henry's friend Don Kava, a part-time employee, found time to visit him often.

"I know where he is, in the flower box near the garden. When I'm there I just say 'Hi' and 'Good morning,'" Kava said. "Henry would just love to be spread out over McGuckin's ... all those tools, all those gadgets... ."[73]

"I'm sure that's happened dozens more times, and we just don't know about it," Doc Dilkes says.

And yes, there really was a wedding in the store. It started as a joke, part of a long — 12 years long — engagement between Randy Richmond and Theresa Blanding. They spent so much time in the store that they vowed if they ever did tie the knot they should hold the nuptials in the tool department. But after Theresa's 25-year-old son said it would never happen — well, game on.

"On the evening of July 21, 2013, with a small band of well-dressed family members and close friends, Randy Richmond and Theresa Blanding walked hand-in-hand down the aisle — aisle 16 in the Tools department that is — the tall, broad-smiling groom sporting a black fedora, the beaming bride with a small vibrant bouquet, and her son Lucian snapping photos in front of them as they strode in sync along the waxed floor lined with circular saws," read a story in Boulder Magazine. The newly wedded couple declared the store a "temple of usefulness and longevity" — and asked for just one thing from those who planned to give gifts: McGuckin gift cards.[74]

And no story about McGuckin's would be complete without celebrities. The store's long roster of famous shoppers includes world-class athletes, musicians, politicians and Hollywood types — and who knows how many drifted through the store unnoticed, given many famous people's penchant for traveling (or trying to travel) incognito? Actress Jane Fonda attempted, but failed, to disguise herself when she visited the store in the 1980s during her son's time at CU-Boulder.

"She was looking around the counter like she was scared or paranoid; she didn't disguise too well," Dee recalls. "They put her with a girl in housewares, Lynn Glinsky" — she of the staticky nylon stockings — "who was good with customers, and Dave told everybody to leave her the heck alone and treat her like a regular customer."

Other actors who strolled the aisles at one time or another include Val Kilmer, who played "Hamlet" at the 1982 Colorado Shakespeare Festival; Eddie Murphy and Bill Murray, who, according to Barry, "came in higher than kites; Dave was telling them jokes and had no idea who they were … or how high they were"; Ann-Margret, Bing Crosby and Slim Pickens, the stars of the 1966 remake of "Stagecoach," filmed at Caribou Ranch west of Boulder; Mariel Hemingway; and Robert Redford when he was a student at CU-Boulder.

"I waited on him. He was very good-looking back then," Dee says, bluntly adding, "before he had kids."

The store has attracted star athletes from local and visiting teams, including Denver Broncos Bucky Dilts, Jake Plummer, Mike Montler and Randy Gradishar; NBA coaching genius Phil Jackson; former CU football coach Rick Neuheisel; and Chauncey Billups, who starred for the Buffaloes before moving on to the NBA.

Boulder being Boulder, and McGuckin's being McGuckin's, superstars from outdoor sports have not just visited the store, but also become regular customers in search of solutions. They include Olympic medal-winner, pro cyclist and Boulder native Davis Phinney and his wife, Connie Carpenter, also an Olympic medalist; cyclist Timmy Duggan; skier Billy Kidd, a former world champion and Olympic silver medalist; world-renowned climber Kevin Donald of Eldorado Springs; Jeff Lowe, owner of numerous first ascents in the Rockies, Alps and Himalayas; Jim Wickwire and Jim Whittaker, the first Americans to summit Mount Everest; Jon Krakauer, author of the outdoor classics "Into the Wild," "Into Thin Air" and many other best-selling nonfiction books; and Boulder's Aron Ralston, best known for cutting off his own arm to save himself when it became pinned in a slot canyon in Utah, subject of his best-seller, "Between a Rock and a Hard Place."

"You mean the best hardware store in the universe?" Ralston enthuses when asked to share his thoughts about McGuckin's. His young son, also a fan, "wears his blue McGuckin's cap nonstop."

In part thanks to Jim Guercio's Caribou Ranch, a long-time recording studio off the Peak to Peak Highway north of Nederland, the store also has seen a parade of famous rock musicians, many who became regulars while living in the Boulder area. The roster includes jazz vocalist and songwriter Harry Connick Jr., who married supermodel Jill Goodacre, a 1982 Fairview High School graduate; James Taylor (though nobody knew it until the singer-songwriter said he was a McGuckin's regular on the air after winning an award from Boulder's "e-Town" radio show); former Jamestown resident Joe Walsh, the late-period Eagles guitarist whose early 1970s song "Rocky Mountain Way" is a much-loved Colorado anthem; Todd Park Mohr, frontman for Big Head Todd and the Monsters; June Carter Cash (legend has it her husband, Johnny Cash, remained outside in the bus, napping); Kris Kristofferson and Rita Coolidge; Richie Furay, founding member of Poco and Buffalo Springfield, now a minister living in Broomfield; the late Dan Fogelberg, who "went to McGuckin's on a regular basis" while he lived in nearby Jamestown[75]; Stephen Stills and Neil Young, both of whom lived in the area (Bruce Ramp recalls when Young's "people" came in to buy 25 metal gas cans during the 1970s oil embargo so he wouldn't run out during a recording session at Caribou); and the late Beach Boys member, Carl Wilson.

"Doc (Dilkes) came up to me one day and said, 'You know who's over there?'" says Bob Perkins, who loved to crank KBCO and sing and dance barefoot while stocking after hours. "I said, 'no,' and he said, 'Carl Wilson of the Beach Boys.' ... I'm not one who goes off looking for autographs, but that day I *had* to go over and talk to him. I asked him if he was finding everything all right and said, 'I really am not a person who likes to infringe on privacy, but I also wanted to say happy birthday.' I only knew because KBCO had announced it that morning. I think he was impressed!"

"We're pretty sure there are countless others who have been in the store because their kid went to CU or they were recording at Caribou, but those are all people a current employee can confirm have shopped at McGuckin's," says marketing manager Louise Garrels.

Of course, any place as useful as McGuckin's has also through the years attracted a less-savory element in search of tools to commit crimes and misdemeanors, at least one of them notorious. And having employed thousands of employees over the years, inevitably some will turn out to have less-than-pure intentions, as when Boulder police arrested four staff members in 1993 for conspiring to get refunds for items they'd stolen from the store.

"The police have been in here many times, including when office people were committing financial crimes," Doc Dilkes says. "But we've also had murders and suicides happen over the decades, and investigators come in to compare items to murder weapons — say a guy commits suicide, and they find a knife with a McGuckin's price tag."

By far the most unwelcome case is the still-unsolved murder of Boulder's 6-year-old JonBenet Ramsey. Investigators literally cordoned off parts of the store as they sought to learn all they could about items found in the child's home on University Hill, where she was found on the morning of Dec. 26, 1996, including duct tape, rope and a wooden paint-brush handle used in the murder. Employees knew exactly what was going on and found the whole thing horrific.

"Yes, somebody came in and bought murder supplies. It's just one tragic thing that happened at McGuckin's, though of course we didn't want to be involved," Doc says. "We don't want that kind of business. Couldn't they have gone to Home Depot that day?"

Home Depot. It's a name that comes up often during conversations with McGuckin employees, who find the corporate home-improvement giant, with its blazing orange logo and aggressive "Let's DO this!" motto, to be the antithesis of everything Bill McGuckin green stands for. Surprisingly, despite the company's move into Louisville in 1996, Home Depot didn't get a foothold in Boulder proper until 2004, where it became the southern anchor for the new Twenty Ninth Street outdoor mall, built on the site of the former Crossroads Mall by Santa Monica, California-based Macerich.

When the new mall was still in the planning phases, Arthur M. Coppola, CEO of Macerich— the same guy who had been trying to get him to move to Crossroads all those years ago — called Dave to say that the company was considering building a Super Target to anchor the south end of Twenty Ninth Street and wondering if McGuckin's would be interested in relocating to the current Target site at 28th and Pearl streets. Dave said, "No thanks." Business was good, and he couldn't see any advantage to moving again. Also, it would just be a big hassle, since that location was a good deal farther than just across the parking lot; there would be no sprightly mini-train moving inventory. Anyway, he didn't like what he perceived as the company's pressure tactics — "They just wanted to get you under their thumb."

The Super Target never happened. Instead, Macerich invited Home Depot to anchor the new mall's south end.

"It's not the worst news in the world," store manager Ray Gralewski told the Daily Camera. "We knew somebody was going in there. … Competition is part of life, and we'll have to do our best to compete."[76]

A 125,000-square-foot Home Depot in Boulder, just a few blocks east, was the biggest of contenders to come along in McGuckin's storied half-century history, a bruising brawler with a piston jab and a mean uppercut. It had put plenty of small independents out of business in its march toward 2,000-plus stores and $20 billion annual sales figures. But McGuckin's had always been fleet, if nothing else, a dancing butterfly in the ring. And around Boulder, even beyond, the crowd was pulling for the underdog, now so well-known that it had become a potent local metaphor.

"We're McGuckin Hardware, not Home Depot, in our approach to business," Dave Wade, co-owner of the upstart, independent Front Range Bank in Lakewood told a business reporter. "Rather than looking for ways to generate income, we look for solutions to customers' problems."[77]

CHAPTER THIRTEEN

McGuckin Labs (un-Inc.)

It's a gold mine of mental improvisation.
— James Balog, photographer and filmmaker

Of all the roles McGuckin Hardware has played in its 60 years, perhaps the most famous is as an incubator of ideas and innovation, a playground for inventors and entrepreneurs, with staff members who eagerly embrace the role of co-conspirator and sometimes, simply cheerleader. McGuckin's may not have scored any patents itself, but generations of inventors credit the store for countless able assists.

"When somebody comes in and says, 'I want to invent something,' I love it. I say, 'Great, cool, let's go,'" Doc Dilkes says.

The late Ran Ransom set the tone for wizardry, enthusiastically jumping in to tailor solutions for any and all customer problems, the more vexatious, the better.

"He would definitely always have an opinion or an answer or a solution, or he would make something up. He'd say, 'I don't know. Let's try it. Let's open it up,'" Doc Dilkes says. "He wouldn't want to work on anything unless he knew all about it. A total inventor, take-it-apart kind of guy."

George Gamow was a Russian immigrant and brilliant physicist who spent much of his illustrious career at CU-Boulder. Along with the late Isaac Asimov, he advanced the cause of science in the American mind through a series of highly accessible books for the lay reader about physics, astronomy, evolution, biology and more. His character Mr. Tompkins guided uncounted thousands of schoolchildren into the world of science in the post-World War II era. He came to Boulder a year after McGuckin's had opened and immediately fell in love with the store.

"He was as clumsy as could be with practical things, but he loved gadgets," says his daughter-in-law Elfriede Gamow. "McGuckin's had all the tools and gadgets. It didn't matter if he needed it, he loved bringing them home even though he never used them."

Constantly in and out of the store, smoking cigarette after cigarette while he roamed the aisles like a kid shaking presents under a Christmas tree, George soon became friends with both Bill McGuckin and Dave Hight.

"He'd park his Mercedes convertible by the store and just come look around. One day he came in looking for a thermometer for the outside of his dog house," Dave says. "I was helping him, and I turned around and there he was with his pants down around his ankles. 'These dommed English pants, I can't keep them up!'"

Though brilliant and cerebral, George was no inventor. But his son Igor, a genuinely memorable character in a town that has produced more than its share, is a different story. Igor quit high school to become a professional ballet dancer in Washington, D.C., where he trod the boards by night and zipped around the city as a motorcycle courier for the Eisenhower administration by day, sometimes with a German shepherd straddling the gas tank. In 1957, he followed his father and mother to Boulder, to enroll at CU.

"I sold all my motorcycles and jackets, everything I had, and decided the academic life might not be all that bad," says Igor, who lives with German-born Elfriede — and their ninth German shepherd — in a quirky stone home hovering above Boulder Creek at the mouth of Boulder Canyon.

Igor finished his undergraduate and graduate studies and was hired to teach biology at his alma mater, but academia did not turn out to be all that great, either. He scuffled with administrators who were trying to shoehorn him into teaching engineering and became embroiled in an alleged sexual-harassment controversy that led to his firing. But CU gave him the opportunity to indulge his inventive side, and he went on to patent a number of inventions.

"People don't believe me, but almost everything I've done, I've done because of my students," Igor says.

Most famous among his inventions is the Gamow Bag, a device that can create high-altitude pressure inside an inflatable chamber — essentially a portable hyperbaric chamber. Now standard equipment for first aid in alpine country, the bag can alleviate symptoms for injured and ill climbers on the slopes of Everest, K2 or Denali.

But that's not what Igor was after when he first started tinkering. He had a student, Jeffrey Drew Gear, who was also a competitive alpine and Nordic skier, who started wondering if he could find a way to condition himself by living at altitude while training as if at sea level. Together, he and Igor built an 8-foot, fabric bubble and pressurized it to two pounds per square inch with a vacuum cleaner, creating the equivalent of atmospheric pressure at sea level. Athletes could then theoretically set up a treadmill inside to train. Igor took out a patent on the invention, but there were few takers, and The Bubble soon burst.

Unfazed, he decided to adapt the concept to a much smaller size, so the chamber could be easily hauled to 20,000 — or 29,000 — feet to help ailing alpinists. The prototype Gamow Bag was essentially a mummy sleeping bag pumped up to sea-level pressure, but it was extremely difficult to get the fabric and seams to hold the air. Enter McGuckin's, where floor staff hooked him up with "a whole bunch of different adhesives" until he found one that worked, and sold him a small plastic C-clamp to tighten and secure the inflation hose in place. Problems solved, Igor earned himself a patent — and the enduring gratitude of alpinists around the world. As one website puts it, "The climbing community seized it as the answer to all their problems. Without altitude sickness they could climb higher, and faster."[78]

After being invited by The American Alpine Club to give a talk on the invention, Igor and Elfriede began making the bags and selling them over the phone. In the late 1980s he sold the invention to DuPont and hasn't needed a "day job" ever since.

"At first they had to work with McGuckin's for all the little pieces," says Igor, now 80. "I had to laugh, here was big DuPont shopping at McGuckin's."

But the Gamow Bag was just the most famous of many patented inventions Igor created with help from McGuckin's. There was the K9 Cooling Jacket, a snug canvas vest designed to keep active dogs cool in hot weather. The idea was to fill the pockets with something that would evaporate and conduct heat away from the body. But it was Ran Ransom who suggested Igor use "hydrogels" — usually placed in flower pots to hold moisture — for the fill.

"When you add water, they expand by 99 percent. So Elfriede was sewing K9 jackets filled with these gel crystals. You'd wet it once and it would keep a dog cool for 24 hours," Igor says. Never as excited by the business end of invention, he marketed the vests for about 15 years before dropping the business.

He also developed a "pressurized snorkel" using parts from McGuckin's, which acted as a kind of underwater Gamow bag, allowing people to stay underwater for long periods of time. He ended up patenting and selling that technology, too, and it now goes by the name of Brownie's Third Lung.

Though few are as prolific at invention as Gamow, many others have turned to McGuckin's for help in solving problems or refining their ideas.

Oscar-nominated filmmaker James Balog says the inventory and expertise at his favorite hardware store literally made his documentary "Chasing Ice" — a seven-year project that vividly demonstrates how climate change is drastically shrinking the planet's glaciers and ice caps — possible. He'd been going crazy trying to find an effective way to mount expensive camera equipment to withstand months of time-lapse photography in the coldest environments on earth.

"We needed to create a solid post that could be bolted to bedrock next to a glacier, on which we would mount the waterproof housing for the cameras," Balog says. "It was basically a fancy carpentry project, but it required a lot of unusual tinkering. The solution wasn't obvious."

But he knew where to start looking for answers. The filmmaker was in and out of McGuckin's practically every day for three months — seeking exactly the right nuts, bolts, washers, caulking, brackets and more. Still, he was stumped by the problem of what kind of material to use for the posts themselves.

"A guy whose name I never even knew who had previously been a machinist for NOAA (the National Oceanic and Atmospheric Administration) was working over there in nuts and bolts. He said, 'What you need is 80/20 extruded aluminum,' because it's rigid, but you can put cavities in it to take the weight down," he says. And that turned out to be the perfect solution, allowing Balog and the film's crew to set up cameras from New Zealand to the Arctic Circle.

Balog, who makes a point of visiting hardware and building-supply stores while traveling the country, says no place comes close to McGuckin's.

"I consider the presence of McGuckin's in our community is absolutely one of the greatest resources we have," he says. "It's a goldmine of mental improvisation."

Most famously, McGuckin's employees love to point out that hardware they've sold is now circling the earth in satellites and scientific instruments, thanks to a long, symbiotic relationship with an aerospace giant that came to town just two years after Bill McGuckin opened the store.

"There's this place down the street you may have heard of, Ball Brothers (the original name; the Boulder operation is known as Ball Aerospace and Technology) that shoots little things into the sky," says buyer John Haskovec. "McGuckin's has hardware going around the Earth, and we're real proud of that. Their people were always in and out of here. They'd come in and say, 'We can't wait for this!' and we'd give 'em our best shot."

Frank Hanks remembers a Ball engineer who came in looking for steel cables of a very specific size that needed to be crimped. Frank hooked him up and even crimped the cables for him, but the guy was strangely dodgy when asked what it was all for.

"He came back a few months later and said, 'Now that it's done I can tell you: Those were safety cables for a $30 million satellite,'" Frank says. "He didn't want to tell me that before we made them."

"McGuckin's was always a key place for us. I never knew of any other hardware store, even in neighboring towns and cities, where you could get the things we needed," says Boulder's Tim Ostwald, who worked in systems at Ball for many decades.

"McGuckin's is an institution," says Ball Aerospace co-founder MercMercure, who left the company in 1980 and started a series of tech-related businesses. "And every other company I've been associated with does the same thing and shops at McGuckin's."

Ball engineers still frequent the store in their quest to help science discover new knowledge about the universe. Ironically, sales of Ball Brothers' first, decidedly low-tech product — the famous Mason jar beloved by jam-makers and moonshiners — are once again a big seller for McGuckin's: "We sell a hundred times more Ball jars than we used to," Earl Duncan says in a half-whisper, "for the marijuana business." Ditto for the booming craft-beer industry and home brewers, who often buy equipment and need to create peripheral products, such as the wooden tap handle designed by Avery Brewing for its Ellie's Nut Brown Ale.

There are far too many stories about assists from "McGuckin Labs" to mention them all, and there are surely many cases of inspiration or assistance that have gone unreported over the decades. The fingerprints of the "McGuckin Lab" can be found everywhere from high-Earth orbit to the sheer granite cliffs of the Italian Alps, a Tokyo window box or a dance studio in New York City. Here are a few less-known examples:

After retiring from her career as a ballerina, Whitney Speer began to teach dance at a housing project in the Chelsea neighborhood of New York City, hoping to offer "real" ballet to local kids. When it came time to mount the barres — bars mounted to the wall for stretching and practicing — she turned to her father, Boulder's Richard Lee Speer, an honorary McGuckin's expert. "He helped me purchase the brass hardware that would hold the ballet barres. I've not been back in many years, but those barres could still be up thanks to

Dave Hight and my dad. … I was always embarrassed about my Dad's hanging around there, but … the Hights and their employees loved my Dad. I'm sure he always had a joke or a story for entertainment's sake."

After Mark Weitzman, who first shopped at McGuckin's as a teenager in the '70s,moved to Tokyo in the late 1990s, the thing he missed the most about Colorado was good, hot Mexican food. When he discovered that you can't buy jalapeño or tomatillo plants in Japan, he went to McGuckin's website and struck up an email conversation with staffer Bob Mulder, who gave him advice on what seeds to buy. "He wrote several paragraphs full of information, (and) when he didn't have exactly what I had asked about, he did some more research," then packed everything up and shipped it off to Weitzman. "All this effort for inexpensive items — the most expensive thing I ordered cost $29.99," says Weitzman. P.S., he adds, "The jalapeño peppers thrived but the tomatillos died."

Former CU engineering student, Ball Brothers employee and part-time McGuckin's salesman EphremGelfman patented "Ephrem's Bottle Cutter," an apparatus to cut the necks off wine, beer and other bottles so the bases can be buffed and used as drinking glasses. Restaurants, including Boulder's famous Cork & Cleaver (today The Cork), had been serving drinks in cut-bottle glasses, but making them was arduous, requiring a rapidly spinning, water-cooled industrial blade. Tinkering in his garage with parts he'd bought at McGuckin's, Gelfman came up with a simple system for amateur use and began selling it at the store. "The rest is history. … I sold out quickly because of the exposure I received — everybody in Boulder shopped at McGuckin's. I'm still, many, many years later, with my own website, selling this product all over the world; I've probably sold 750,000 bottle cutters since then, (and) it all started from a sample placement at the checkout counter at McGuckin's."

When trainer Allen Lim was developing what would become Boulder-based Skratch Labs' Secret Drink Mix to "optimize performance and life" for athletes, he found he couldn't get a thorough stir with just a wooden spoon and a five-gallon bucket. So he started taking test batches down to McGuckin's, where the staff allowed him to shake things up with their mechanical paint agitators.

In 1992, when the staff finally got up the nerve to ask world-class rock climber Kevin Donald why he was in and out of the store looking for a drill that would penetrate rock, they learned he had been training actor Sylvester Stallone for the 1993 film "Cliffhanger" in the famous Dolomites of Italy, and the production team lacked an effective rock drill. "Back in the day, there was a two-stroke, chainsaw-driven hammer drill," Barry Hight says. "So we found one and ordered it for him, bits and all."

Daniel Haarburger, a Boulder native and recent graduate of Stanford University, knew just where to look when he started building a prototype for a Kickstarter-funded project to build a device to help people with broken bones walk — the beloved, gadget- and gear-stuffed aisles of his favorite store as he was growing up. "When I started prototyping, I went back to McGuckin," he told Inc. magazine. "And, of course, they jumped in and gave me a hand." If anything, he was even more tickled to come across another of his inventions, which attaches a cellphone to a bike handlebar, on sale. "Going into the childhood store I loved and seeing the Handleband on the wall — that made it for me."[79]

Inventory and invention. It's tempting to give all the credit for the "McGuckin Lab" to Dave Hight's buying philosophy.

"They have everything. Literally everything. Those guys have one of everything, and they know where it is. McGuck's leads you to want to move to Boulder," says Steve Garran, chief creator at Club Workshop, a Denver makerspace —a community workspace where artists, computer and technology geeks, scientists and others come together to socialize and collaborate.[80]

But just as important is another linchpin of the McGuckin Way: relationships.

Rick Case, founder and CEO of NiteIze, a Boulder company that makes and markets LED lighting solutions for outdoor recreation, patented tools for campers, specialty shoelaces and much more, was a CU student in 1989 when he approached McGuckin's about selling his first invention — the Flashlight Friend, an elastic band that turned a Mini Maglite flashlight into a headlamp. Today, NiteIze ships globally and is one of the biggest employers in Boulder County. McGuckin's has long sent new collaborators and inventors the company's way, resulting in such unique products as the Steelie, a magnetic car-phone mount, and the Inka Mobil, a write-everywhere pen and stylus.

"Dave and Barry know everybody. Barry is a connector, the kind of guy who puts people and their vast brain resources together. He's passionate in his commitment to so many people; he's excited, and it's contagious. He got that from his dad," Case says. "McGuckin's is an advocate for local business and entrepreneurs. They allow inventors to display their products. That's what they are all about. They are a great community resource."

CHAPTER FOURTEEN

The McGuckin Way

Dave's first rule is old and simple: Treat people the way you would like to
be treated.

— Bob Perkins, employee since 1980

Throughout this book it's been referred to as the McGuckin Way, but others have different names for the way Dave and Dee Hight — and earlier, Bill McGuckin — have insisted on running their remarkably enduring, unique business for the past six decades. Employees who hire on sometimes hear it described as "being McGuckinized" and exchange knowing looks at the expression McGuckin U, as in University.

Bottom line, there is a way, a philosophy, a set of values and ethics that have stood McGuckin Hardware in good stead since its earliest days, allowing the business to throw even the biggest, baddest competitor against the ropes, or at least hold its own in the ring.

But what *is* the McGuckin Way, exactly? It is, as they say, complicated. The minute you try to sum it up — it's customer service, a willingness to keep inventory, treating employees right so they want to stay and can afford to raise families and move ahead in life — you've sold it short.

"I call it the 'grandpa attitude,'" Doc Dilkes says, after 37 years at the store. "Be friendly. Treat everyone like a neighbor. That's how it started, when everyone was Bill McGuckin's neighbor. ... A family-owned hardware store like McGuckin's is one of the last, great pieces of Americana in business. We epitomize that."

"It's really all the store has got going for it: service and inventory and a homey atmosphere," Frank Hanks says. "Without that edge, I don't think there would still be a McGuckin's."

Many self-proclaimed experts have swooped in over the years to advise McGuckin's on what it's "doing wrong" or tut-tut over the fact that the operation allegedly isn't up to today's business standards.

"I remember some kid who had been taking business courses at CU coming in and saying, 'You know, I hate to tell you this, but you are doing it all wrong,'" Frank Hanks says with a wry smile. "He said we couldn't possibly be surviving and that we'd be out of business soon enough."

The McGuckin Way, like some ancient monastic practice, is simple but sometimes subtle; layered, yet apparent to anyone who shops or works at the store. If you had to catalog its key tenets, it might go something like this:

Price

Might as well start with the big, green elephant in the room, the frequent charge from corporate competitors that McGuckin's is "overpriced." First off, it ain't necessarily so, as many shoppers have found.

"I bought my Old Hickory paring knife (at McGuckin's) in about 1973 — still using it today," says writer N.C. Weil, who grew up in Boulder, attended the University of Colorado and now lives in Denver. "And a few years ago I was able to buy a new White Mountain ice cream freezer (at a) lower price than from Target or the White Mountain factory at McGuckin's, and in stock now, no shipping. Can't beat that!"

And of course, sometimes the advertised prices of competitors don't actually turn out to be the deal customers thought they were.

"It's a bait-and-switch. They'll sell, say, a roll of tape for $2.77. The consumer walks in and sees we are selling it for $4.99 and complains," Barry Hight explains. "But see, that's a 20-yard roll, which we can't buy, and there's hardly anything on the roll. We're selling them a commercial roll, which is actually a better deal."

Over the years, many contractors have learned that sending someone down to McGuckin's is the most efficient way to buy supplies, in both time and money. "You send your guy down, he's in and out with everything he needs, instead of sending him running around for two or three hours. You end up paying for that," Frank Hanks says.

But it would be a mistake to get the idea that McGuckin's is defensive about its pricing. Indeed, many of the store's prices *are* higher than those of its corporate and online competitors. It's just that in the McGuckin Way, price isn't everything; Dave Hight doesn't do "loss leaders."

"Walmart will sell 700 key items below cost for a year, just to dominate the market," Dave says. "People have now been taught to buy for price only, not principles, as if that's all that matters. Well, I think they should buy for principles, too."

Principles like paying your employees not just a "fair wage," but enough to raise families, buy homes, improve their lives and contribute to the community themselves. Contrast that to large, national companies that openly strive to limit employees' hours to ensure they don't have to pay benefits and deliberately pay them so little that many workers literally couldn't survive without help from the government. Walmart's low-wage workers, for example, cost taxpayers an estimated $6.2 billion annually for public assistance, including subsidized housing, food stamps and Medicaid; a single Walmart Super Center can cost taxpayers between $900,000 and $1.75 million a year.[81] The six heirs of Sam Walton's family fortune, meanwhile, were worth $152 billion in 2014, the same as the bottom 42 percent of all Americans combined.[82]

Garrison Keillor's long-running radio program "A Prairie Home Companion," which first aired in 1974, each week features "The News From Lake Wobegon," a folksy, often funny, segment about the goings-on in a small Minnesota town. In "Lake Wobegon Days," a 1986 collection of stories and history about the fictional town, Keillor makes a spirited, comical defense of family-owned businesses.

Lake Wobegon is served by Ralph's Pretty Good Grocery. When Ralph's sister-in-law serves him fish bought from the massive, new Higgledy-Piggledy grocery store in nearby St. Cloud, the disgusted grocer observes that if everyone sneaks off to the gigantic corporate store in search of slightly lower prices and exotic selection, little Lake Wobegon is doomed. No businesses, no jobs, no money, no town.

"If people were to live by comparison shopping the town would go bust," Keillor writes, and loyalty to your neighbors means shopping at local Clifford's Eyewear instead of buying fancy Calvin Klein frames from Vanity Vision in St. Cloud because, "Calvin Klein isn't going to come with the Rescue Squad and he isn't going to teach your children about redemption by grace. You couldn't find Calvin Klein to save your life."[83]

"It isn't all about price, and it shouldn't be. No two stores should have the same prices because they don't have the same overhead, the same customers, the same community," Dave Hight says. "And if all you care about is the lowest prices, you've got to sacrifice something. People are still having to pay. Our business is making a great living for 260 souls, and that's not even talking about vendors. ... When customers come to me to complain about prices I explain,

'Hey, we've got benefits for our people, and we should pay 'em right, don't you think, since you aren't going to tip them in a hardware store.'"

John Haskovec flatly declares, "I'm proud of the prices we charge for our goods at McGuckin's. It's hard to pay the employees and keep the kind of staff we have around with the competition, not just Home Depot, but the Internet. Sometimes we can't *buy* an item for what it's *selling* on the Internet, with free shipping. But we're giving better service and employing more people," he says. "I think the new American ethic is everyone wants to have more, but pay less, and what we've lost is the idea of giving service."

Quality

Most Americans probably don't realize it, but in their relentless pursuit of the lowest price, they may be contributing to the decline in quality of the goods they buy.

Worse, the market power of enormous retailers focused on profit maximization for shareholders inevitably translates into a short-term focus.

"Because manufacturers now depend on a few large chains for such a big portion of their business, chains exert enormous pressures to drive down costs. And they can only do that so much by eliminating a few middle managers. Pretty soon, they have no choice but to start pitching shoddy products," says Jeff Milchen, co-director of the American Independent Business Alliance. "People don't appreciate the degree to which a few giant chains and Amazon are depreciating product quality."

Dave and Barry Hight have seen that downward cycle, and they don't like it. The days when they could offer mostly American-made goods are long gone, because of large-scale economic changes that have seen much manufacturing move overseas. But they believe McGuckin's shoppers, at least, are willing to pay a premium to buy top-of-the-line products that work well and last a long, long time. Just like Bill McGuckin, who stocked expensive but durable Mercury boat engines.

"We have one line now, Festool out of Germany, that makes really expensive tools. But they are 10 times as good as anyone else's," Dave says. Home Depot, in contrast, has acquired names of once-high-quality products — Behr paint and Ridgid tools, for example — then slapped them on inferior goods.

"One of the things we are trying to do at AMIBA is to get Americans to distinguish between cheapness and value. American culture is so obsessed with cheapness that it's often at the expense of value," Milchen says. "In the past few decades, for example, the expected lifespan of a refrigerator, TV or lawnmower is down the toilet. It may cost less upfront, but it costs a hell of a lot more in the long run." Buyers have to replace products more often, and there is "a huge environmental cost to the fact that appliances are now literally built to be disposable."

McGuckin's success, Milchen argues, is almost entirely due to the company's attention to *quality*. Quality employees who offer quality expertise on a huge inventory of quality items that, in many cases, have been specifically requested by customers interested in … quality.

"McGuckin's makes an investment in selling quality merchandise," he says. "The Home Depots and Lowe's of the world are so focused on price and continually hammering suppliers for a lower price that they are sacrificing user-friendliness, even the safety of their customers."

Inventory

Dave Hight readily admits he pays through the nose for his approach to inventory, which even Bill McGuckin eyed warily back in the 1960s, given that he has to pay taxes on items in stock. These days, "Just in Time" or "JIT" — stocking goods only when "needed"— is the inventory strategy of choice for minions of spreadsheet-addicted management-school graduates to "improve efficiency."

But the question is, *whose* efficiency? Certainly not the customer's, as Frank Hanks has experienced all too often in retirement. Frank and Joann live on a small farm east of Niwot, where they put up hay and have raised a few beef cattle. Often as not these days, when Frank heads to the tractor dealership looking for a part, he comes home empty-handed. Even if he calls ahead, he's likely to get a recording or worse, put on hold or told he'll have to call back later because another customer just walked in.

"They don't have any inventory, and not much service," he says. "The guy says he can order it. No, I just want to come here, to your store, pick it up right now and use it. I end up having to order stuff online because nobody carries it. The guy assures me he can get it for me in three days; well, I can get it in two days online if I have to."

At McGuckin's, not only is it the practice to order whatever the customer wants, but also a long-standing policy to let them buy in whatever quantity they need, not what serves the company's convenience or bottom line. It helps to have a vast, local warehouse — a 100-by-450-foot facility on the former site of Beech Aircraft north of Boulder, which the company bought in 1998 and now operates as McGuckin Distribution (as Hight Enterprises, the family also owns another warehouse on Sterling Place in east Boulder). Under its original owner, the Beech warehouse, 100 feet wide and 450 feet long, made quiet history, X-raying the failed engines from Apollo 13 and serving as a fueling station for the U.S. military's SCUD missiles until 2000.

"When we took over the property we remodeled the whole place," Barry says. "One day after work we stood at one end and someone said, 'Hey boss, look, you can see the curvature of the earth in the floor. It looks like the warehouse from the end of 'Raiders of the Lost Ark.'"

"If you only need one widget, you can buy one and not have to buy a package of 12" as at so many corporate stores, says engineer Robert LaRue.

"McGuckin's always has every little widget I can't find anywhere else," says Boulder's Karen Eifler. "I also love the bulb selection in the spring and fall. I pick out one of this and one of that and end up with a fabulous array of spring flowers."

"We stock over one million fasteners, but I'm happy to sell you a single nail or screw," Barry Hight says.[84]

That's exactly how it should be, Dave Hight believes.

"You should just be able to walk in when you need it, a light bulb, a spade, anything you need, and we're going to have it or order it for you right there," he says. "McGuckin's has never been about trying to sell people things. What we want to sell is what people need."

Service

When Boulder's Nancy Wrigglesworth showed up for her very first job as a sales clerk at Mountain Sports, she expected she'd have to go through some training. But she sure didn't expect where she'd be told to start.

"The owner, Bob Swartz, told us to go to McGuckin's to study their customer service," she recalls. "They were — and are — amazing."

McGuckin's Hardware has long been held up as a kind of gold standard in how to treat customers, and it started right from the beginning.

"Dave always wanted customers waited on as soon as they come in the door, so everybody stood at the register. As soon as someone came in, you'd walk up to him. You'd help him find what he needed, ring him up, and take his purchases out to the car," Frank Hanks recalls.

As the Shopper Culture website puts it, "They know their audience and cater to them. They deliver what their competitors can't. And they are thoroughly local."[85]

Many an "efficiency expert" or theory-minded business professor no doubt sniffs at the number of staff that Dave insists work the floor. But customers who have experienced a long, lonely vigil while waiting for help in some cavernous home-improvement discount center surely prefer walking into McGuckin's and being immediately greeted by someone eager to answer their questions and send them to the right expert in the right department.

"What it boils down to is that we've got a good thing going here at McGuckin's because of what Dave instilled in us about our customers," says sales staffer Earl Duncan, who has been with the store since 1974. "They are not just our loyal customers; they are our friends. We treat them like their time is valuable, and they keep coming back."

Community

Growing up on farms and in small towns in the Midwest, including Brighton and Fort Lupton (Colorado may be considered a Western state, but both culturally and geographically, much of it actually belongs to the Midwest and Southwest), both Donna Mae McGuckin and David Keith Hight learned the importance of community. When a blizzard roared down from the north on Rudolph, Nebraska, or a tornado blew through Blackwell, Oklahoma, you needed to be able to rely on your neighbors. And if your neighbors didn't patronize your business, no one would, so you wanted to treat them right.

But as Dave often points out, you don't treat friends like you're just trying to sell them something. You owe them, and the community at large, *more* than they owe you. Boulder embraced the McGuckin Way starting in 1955 and has provided an unimaginably bounteous life for two families with such hardscrabble beginnings and a living for hundreds of employees. For that reason, Dave and Dee have long supported community causes and helped put many businesses and people on the road to success.

They have generously supported a wide range of events and organizations, including BIBA, the Little Britches Rodeo, the Humane Society of Boulder Valley, CU Presents — which offers performing arts programs on campus — Safehouse Progressive Alliance's annual Chocolate Lovers' Fling, the Boulder Jaycees, the Emergency Family Assistance Association, Little League teams, Boulder Flood Relief and more.

McGuckin's has been the mother of invention for entrepreneurs and served as silent partner in many Boulder businesses over the years. The Hights also have taken a more visible role in jumpstarting many local businesses, including RallySport, Cherokee Data Systems and Boulder's Dinner Theatre (now BDT Stage), contributing to the employment of thousands of local residents who have never donned the green vest.

Boulder Mayor Susan Osborne may have declared Dec. 8, 2009, Dave Hight Day, in recognition of his community spirit and philanthropy, but as Dave readily acknowledges, Dee, Bill McGuckin, all those dedicated employees over the years, indeed, the business itself, all deserve just as much of the credit (of course, that would have made for a rather unwieldy proclamation). Dave also served as a proxy for all those people when he was inducted into the Boulder County Business Hall of Fame in 2006. He and Dee were presented with the Franny Reich Business Hero Award from the Boulder Chamber of Commerce in 2014, in recognition of their roles as "great partners in addressing community needs throughout their years in business, both through the services their store provides and the many contributions they make to community causes."[86]

It's hard to overstress how critical the idea of supporting local business and thus, the community at large, is to the McGuckin Way. Dave and Barry have respectfully disagreed with the Boulder Chamber of Commerce's boosterism for big-box stores and efforts to entice corporate chains to come to a city that has demonstrated again and again it will uplift and support local businesses.

"The chamber has its own way of seeing things and likes any kind of business to come to town. We're part of BIBA, and we want people to shop local, we want that money to stay in our community, not go to Atlanta," Barry says.

Boulder is something of a rarity in contemporary America, a place with both the resources and community spirit to stand against the worst excesses of the new cookie-cutter economy, where every city looks the same — endlessly repeating strips of corporate fast-food restaurants and chain stores of every variety. It may surprise those who insist that's "just how it is" to learn that independent businesses have been staging some interesting comebacks in more than one industry in recent years.

"Independent bookstores have been making a resurgence, having outlasted Borders and every other chain except Barnes & Noble, and are holding their own against Amazon. And microbreweries continue to steal market share from big breweries," says AMIBA's Milchen. "People want that community character."

"Fair Trade"

Like any successful business owner, Dave Hight is ever attuned to the subject of politics as it affects his business, especially taxes and regulation. Although he and Dee describe themselves as conservative, the McGuckin

Way appeals to people across the political spectrum. In the age of corporate conglomerates, big-money politics, offshore tax shelters and billionaire owners threatening to move their professional sports teams unless local voters agree to generous tax subsidies, the McGuckin Way is rooted in the kind of economic populism that spurred the post-World War II economic expansion.

Dave quotes the great conservative, Winston Churchill, who, when Britain was facing an influx of cheap goods from far-flung corners of the empire in the late 19th century, said he advocated "fair trade" over "free trade."[87] For Dave, "fair" means that the government and tax code don't favor one scale of business or ownership class — i.e., leviathan conglomerates or online behemoths — over any other, namely, small, locally owned and family-owned businesses.

"Walmart uses the tax code to put everybody out of business," says Dave, usually with the help of government and eager-beaver chambers of commerce who don't distinguish between "jobs" and "good jobs." He notes, for example, the city of Lafayette, Colorado, gave the company a $5 million subsidy, funded by sales taxes, just to open a store. "I just underwent an audit, and if I stole $5 million out of sales tax, I'd be in jail."

Dave argues there are other ways the tax code unfairly burdens private- and family-owned independent businesses. "The corporation doesn't have to pay an inheritance tax because it never dies!" he says; having to pay taxes on inventory as a "current asset"; and the fact that corporate stores are never going to be audited by local tax officials, to name just a few. Meanwhile, enormous corporations and billionaires rack up huge profits but work hard to avoid paying the taxes to build the infrastructure they use and social-safety nets needed by their poorly paid employees. Walmart is one of the 30 American companies with the most profits "booked offshore" (62 percent) to avoid paying taxes that support everything from the military to national parks.[88]

What bothers Dave most is that this is all perfectly legal in a system where money means influence, and influence means never having to say you're sorry for letting noncorporate business owners and private citizens pay more than their fair proportion of the tax burden.

"Hell, I'm not even against Walmart. But we should all have the same rules, and we don't," Dave says. "That's why everyone says, 'Start a chain, get your money out of it, pay yourself these huge salaries.'"

But he'll never do that. Like musicians Willie Nelson, Neil Young and John Mellencamp, whose annual Farm Aid concerts have raised money for family farms since 1985, Dave and Dee Hight simply believe that local, family-owned businesses are the best way to create and sustain healthy communities.

Walmart did eventually muscle its way into Boulder, but only with an ironically named "Neighborhood Market" grocery store, right where Gibson's Discount Center rolled into town in 1965 with big ideas of putting McGuckin's out of business. People shop there, but for Boulder residents who embrace local businesses, to do so would be a kind of betrayal. When the store opened Oct. 1, 2013, Walmart managers said some 1,000 shoppers passed through its doors.[89] But the Coalition for Environmental & Social Responsibility in Boulder also held an all-day "Unwelcome Party" at the site, and around the lunch hour, an unexpected, but very welcome, guest showed up: long-time McGuckin's manager Randy "Doc" Dilkes.

"He went over there just to see what was going on. He walks up in his green vest and the waters *parted*," Dave says. "They started shouting, 'McGuckin's is here, they are going to stand with us!' They were disappointed when he walked right into the store, but Doc just wanted to see what it was about."

Dave has always been proud to pay his taxes — in fact, it's a cornerstone of the McGuckin Way — to support infrastructure and strengthen local communities, from roads to schools to fire and police departments. But under current law, online retailers are off the hook; their customers are supposed to voluntarily calculate and pay state and local sales taxes, but unsurprisingly, virtually none do. Large chains and corporations pay lobbyists to tilt the tax code in their favor and find ways to squirrel profits away in offshore accounts.

"There are real systemic problems — corporate subsidies, tax loopholes — that are playing a huge role in driving the destruction of independent businesses," says AMIBA's Milchen. "Sales tax in Colorado is about 7 percent. In a competition between two businesses, if you give one (the brick-and-mortar retailer) a 7 percent handicap out of the gate in a trade where margins are extremely thin to begin with, that's a huge unfair advantage."

People often aren't even aware of the consequences of buying tax-free online. Tickled pink to have saved a few bucks, Milchen says they have just removed that same amount of revenue from local and state government coffers.

"When people are going online to save a buck or two, it's still coming out of their pocket," he adds. "If the sales taxes aren't there, then fees are higher, property taxes are higher, or services fall apart."

"I'm competing with Amazon.com, which doesn't have to pay all that (tax)," Dave says. "I'd rather all business be owned locally, because when you are owned locally, everyone is equal, subject to the same tax code. That's one way you keep a community strong. And when you support local merchants in Boulder, they all pay property taxes and sales taxes."

Longtime members of the Republican Party, both Dave and Dee say part of the answer is a fair tax code, specifically, a flat tax with an exemption of the first $35,000 — "That's a working guy; he shouldn't have to pay anything," Dave says — and no loopholes for anyone. He's no fan of the Affordable Care Act, aka Obamacare, as much as anything because it's a symptom of how far the country has fallen away from "fair play." The complicated law was, he says, mostly a sop to enormous insurance companies eager to preserve their profits and overhead. Health care and insurance, he says, are a bellwether for much deeper problems in an American economy where the gap between the haves and have-nots is widening precipitously.

"Obamacare wasn't for the working man," he says. "If people had a good job and were paid a decent wage, (they) could afford health care."

Like any traditional economic conservative, Dave is concerned about the size of federal government and believes that many well-intentioned laws and programs have actually made things more difficult for average, working people. Some McGuckin's employees who have witnessed such changes over the years agree. Earl Duncan, for example, always liked having the option of working as much as he wanted, without being sent home because he was incurring overtime.

"In the early days, I worked two shifts every day, 12 or 15 hours a day sometimes, seven days a week," he says. "It was hard, being married and having kids, but it enabled me to save enough to buy a home in Boulder. And I was given the choice to work as much as I wanted."

Dave, to his credit, doesn't run around broadcasting his politics — indeed, it's hard to draw him into such a conversation. He was raised to believe you obeyed the law, and if you didn't like the law, then you should work to change it. And despite the sharp-edged tribalism and often brutal partisanship that characterizes so much public interaction in contemporary America, where millions of people seem to believe they should insult, label, even despise, anyone who doesn't share their beliefs, that is not, never has been, and never will be the McGuckin Way.

"Dave's first rule is old and simple: Treat people the way you would like to be treated," says long-time manager Bob Perkins. "And Dee, God love her, she still comes in and even though she's overwhelmed by all the people, she knows every one of us, and a lot of our families."

Dave sometimes suggests that McGuckin Hardware might not make it in most cities. "Thank heavens a lot of people in Boulder are service-minded and understand what we're trying to do." But J.J. Johnson, executive director of

BIBA, makes the case that the McGuckin Way would play in any town where people care about their community.

"In my experience with Dave, he always exemplifies passion for doing the right thing and practices community stewardship. (McGuckin's) reinvests their profits back into the community; they appreciate that the taxes they pay support such things as our schools, city infrastructure, open space and bike paths," Johnson says. "As Dave has noted, 'Support the things that make your life better, then you're supporting your community through taxes.' So what's important to Dave and Dee Hight? Being plugged into the community, meeting and greeting customers, building friendships, tailoring store inventory to the needs of Boulder, providing service extraordinaire, appreciating loyal employees — some staff have been there 30 to 40 years — giving back to community, and so much more."[90]

"My grandparents never let us forget our great-grandfather (Bill McGuckin), who I never met. He was always in it for the people," says Jason Hight.

"Sixty years for a hardware store is pretty good," says Frank Hanks. "If it hadn't been for Dave, they'd have been gone long ago."

The Golden Rule. Fair play. A refusal to compromise values. Investing in the community. Maybe that's all there is to the McGuckin Way.

Simple, perhaps, but anything but easy.

CHAPTER FIFTEEN

Sixty Years and Counting

We don't let anyone control us because what works for shareholders is not necessarily what works for the people.
— Jason Hight, assistant manager, fourth-generation McGuckin

For Dave and Dee's three sons and eight grandchildren, growing up around McGuckin Hardware was almost as good as having Willie Wonka's factory or Disneyland in their backyard.

"It was like going to the playground when we'd come to visit Dad," says Jason Hight, now 32. "When we'd come in after hours he'd let us rip around the aisles on all the toys. We'd put on Rollerblades and a couple of times rode electric scooters. Whenever my mom would take us kids (Jason and sisters Holly and Mallory) to the store it was like a field trip to Elitch's" — Denver's old Elitch Gardens amusement park.

The store was so huge it was like a world unto itself.

"The shelves were so high, and the back-stock shelves were 10 feet above those, floor to ceiling. Being so small, it was impossible to wrap your head around all the inventory," Jason says. "No matter how many times we came in, we found new stuff all over the place."

He's always enjoyed working at the store, too (what 12-year-old wouldn't want a good, paying job, even if it was "technically not legal"?) right through middle and high school before graduating.

But by the time he graduated, Jason was ready to try life beyond the confines of family. Far from objecting, Barry and Vicki Hight believed so strongly in the importance of seeing the world and gaining experience and independence that they supported their children who chose to go to college out of state. Jason took the opportunity and ran — eight years in Bozeman, Montana, for college (and fishing … and skiing), back to Boulder to work with a cousin in landscaping, a brief stint at McGuckin's, then off to Portland, Oregon, "chasing a girl."

"I never did see myself coming back," he says.

Around Boulder County, people often talk of "Niwot's Curse." Niwot, the Southern Arapaho Indian chief who befriended early settlers in Boulder County, was killed alongside some 150 peaceful women, children and elders by 700 members of the Colorado Territorial Militia in the notorious 1864 Sand Creek Massacre. His eponymous, apocryphal curse says children born (or raised) in Boulder Valley are doomed to return there to live, no matter their grand plans. In Jason's case, the "curse" can only be seen as a blessing. He caught up to that girl he was chasing and moved back to Colorado, her own home state, and they planned to marry in July 2015. And though he didn't expect to come back to the family business, when offered a job, it dawned on him that there's no place he'd rather be.

"Over the years I've realized not only do I love it here, but I consider myself pretty good," he says.

The blood of a new, younger generation will be crucial to keeping McGuckin Hardware thriving and competitive in the new century. Even after six decades of impressive resilience, the McGuckin Way faces a cultural challenge that dwarfs the competitive threat of a single corporation or even an online giant like Amazon.com: The buying habits of younger Americans whose economic lives have been dominated by corporate chains and who have never known a world where they couldn't buy anything they wanted with a click of a mouse.

"Even now, and it will be more so with future generations, everything is so now, now, now," Jason observes. "You go to the movies and something has to blow up in the first 30 seconds."

Jason's sister Mallory has found, to her dismay, that she is often the only student in her business program at Colorado State University who has any conception of why people should support locally owned businesses instead of online or at a big-box store. She tells Barry, "Dad, I feel like I'm so out of step with everyone."

The advent of the YouTube instruction video has been both a blessing and a curse for do-it-yourselfers and the neo-motto "five seconds on Google," or simply FSOG — a snarky Internet generation put-down of anyone who seeks help from humans — have devalued expertise. Never mind if any of the information you may find online is correct. Actual experts are so, you know, 20th century.

Barry tells the story of a customer who had seen a YouTube video instructing him to set a toilet using caulk.

"I said, 'You *saw* that?' and asked him a bunch of questions: Did you do the tile? Is the floor plywood or concrete?" he says.

The man didn't know answers, so Barry explained that you don't want to caulk the toilet to the floor because if the bowl ring leaks, you won't know it until it's too late, and it can ruin the floor beneath. The man insisted that the caulk would protect the floor from, well, dribbles and spray.

"My mama taught me to stand close to the bowl," Barry replied, and the two shared a laugh. The man went away, did it the way Barry advised, and came back later to say, "You guys are really good."

And just about anyone who has picked up a phone at McGuckin's over the past decade has gotten a bemusing call from some poor customer on a cellphone from Home Depot, "Do you have three-way switches? Can you help me solve my problem? There's nobody here to help,'" Barry says, smirking and shaking his head. "And I'll say, 'You know, wiring those three-ways is a dicey thing. Why don't you come over here, and we'll help you.'"

But just about everyone involved with the store — Barry now runs the store, though Dave comes in just about every day — recognizes that to thrive for another 60 years, McGuckin Hardware must both hold onto values that have served it so well and adapt to new technologies and media platforms, not to mention the ever-changing habits of the American consumer.

"Grandpa loves coming in and walking the aisles to see everything is going well, and it's my number-one job to keep him happy," Jason says, smiling. "But we know we have to get more into the online game."

Jason believes McGuckin's can successfully marry the online shopping experience with hands-on shopping at the store and consulting with experts.

"We have to be competitive in price for when people go online. But here, they can also come in and actually see all those humidifiers working. When people buy something online and they run into a problem, they are screwed," he says. "Here, you can come in the next day to talk about what went wrong, and we're going to take care of you, get you a different one or switch models."

Nobody is standing still. The store added Google Wallet and Apple Pay to its payment option in 2015 and has embraced social media in a big way. Unlike those of so many other businesses, McGuckin's Facebook page is much more than a series of yawn-inducing advertisements. Some 14,000 friends regularly visit for the latest news on "Upcycling" — converting waste materials or defunct items into new products or gearing them to new, aesthetic purposes —a Bonfils Blood Center drive at the store or a lesson in how to milk a coconut from "Green Vest Sarah." A true community forum, the page has become a vital bulletin board during local emergencies. During the catastrophic 2013 floods, marketing communication specialist Steve Wilke went on Denver's 9News to share "MacGyver Moments," tips from chin-up McGuckin's Facebook friends on how to repurpose common items — from yoga mats to bags of potting soil to roach killer — for flood mitigation.

At the same time, the store vigorously continues to improve and expand even its most beloved traditions, including the semi-annual Tent Sale, which just gets bigger and better and more popular. As Boulder resident Ed Kahn jestingly observed during the May 2015 sale, "Overheard at McGuckin's: We're gonna need a bigger tent."

"McGuckin's is staying true to its values, keeping personal relationships with employees and suppliers, while making sure they are on top of the game in terms of modernization, maintaining effective, mobile-friendly websites and social media," says Milchen of the American Independent Business Alliance. "They understand that they can't get by on old-school values alone any more."

Things will continue to change, of course. But talk to anybody at McGuckin Hardware, and they'll tell you they expect it to survive and thrive for another 60 years, refusing to back down from any and all challengers — just like pugnacious Dave Hight in his youth.

"Growing up, I remember hearing Dad already talking about the competition in town. In the '60s he'd come home a little frustrated on Mondays and say, 'If somebody will give me a nickel, they can have the place,'" Barry says. "In the '70s that turned into a dime, and in the '80s, a quarter. It was my first lesson in inflation over time."

But through it all, the McGuckin Way has always won out: Dave and Dee could have quit, but they stayed in business to serve customers, so they could enjoy their lives, and everyone at McGuckin's could enjoy theirs. Otherwise, what was the point?

"Dad's dream was always to own a store in a small town," Barry says. "Well, this town grew bigger, and so did the store. More than he ever thought it would."

But none of that has ever gone to Dave's head. Over the years, countless "experts" have advised him to translate McGuckin's success into selling franchises or opening stores in other cities— you know, go for the *big* money; it's the American Way. But Dave always replied that he'd rather someone *else* start a business, and he'd happy to share everything he knows.

For free. No lawyers. No consulting fees. The *McGuckin* Way.

"There are some 30,000 small towns in America," Dave says. "I think we ought to have 30,000 hardware stores, owned by 30,000 families."

Sources

Carnegie Branch for Local History, Boulder Public Library.

Bradbury, Ray. "Dandelion Wine." New York: Doubleday, 1957.

Fetter, Richard. "Frontier Boulder." Boulder: Johnson Books, 1983.

Gannett, Henry. "The Origin of Certain Place Names in the United States." U.S. Government Printing Office, Washington, D.C., 1905

Harvey, Robert. "Amache: The Story of Japanese Internment in Colorado During World War II." Dallas: Taylor Trade Publishing, 2003.

Keillor, Garrison. "Lake Wobegon Days." New York: Penguin, 1986.

Lambrecht, Mona, and the Boulder History Museum. "Images of America: Boulder 1859-1919." Boulder: Arcadia Publishing, 2008.

Meier, Thomas J. "Ed Tangen, The Pictureman: A Photographic History of the Boulder Region, Early Twentieth Century." Boulder: Boulder Creek Press, 1994.

Pettem, Sylvia. "Boulder: A Sense of Time and Place." Longmont: The Book Lode, 2000.

Pettem, Sylvia. "Boulder: Evolution of a City." Boulder: University Press of Colorado, 2006.

Scarnes, John. "Scarnes' New Complete Guide to Gambling." New York: Fireside, 1986.

Schoolland, J.B. "Boulder in Perspective: From Search for Gold to the Gold of Research." Boulder: Johnson Publishing, 1980.

Schoolland, J.B. "Boulder Then and Now." Boulder: Pruett Press, 1967.

Smith, Phyllis. "A Look at Boulder: From Settlement to City." Boulder: Pruett Publishing, 1981.

Voynick, Stephen M. "Climax: The History of Colorado's Climax Molybdenum Mine." Missoula: Mountain Press, 1996.

Waldo, Anna Lee. "Prairie: The Legend of Charles Burton Irwin and the Y6 Ranch." New York: Berkley, 1986.

About the author

Clay Bonnyman Evans grew up in Boulder, Colorado, where he began roaming the hills and mountains beneath the Flatirons with friends — no adult supervision; none needed — starting at age 6. He grew up rock-climbing, bicycling, caving and exploring Colorado's wild places, and at age 15 undertook a 1,200-mile bike ride from Wyoming to Vancouver, Canada, with two friends — no adult supervision; none needed.

After graduating from Boulder High School, where he got his first taste of journalism writing and editing for The Owl, he embarked upon a checkered college career that took him to Columbia University, Colorado College (where he held a party for friends who helped him move into the dorms, then packed up the next day without ever attending a single class) and the University of Colorado-Boulder. He did eventually stop moving long enough to earn degrees from the University of Wyoming and the University of California, Santa Cruz, with majors in agriculture and politics, respectively.

Somewhere in there he took a six-and-a-half-year hiatus to work as a cowboy around the West, including Wyoming, New Mexico, Montana and California. He began his journalism career working nights at the Santa Cruz Sentinel (and got a lesson in journalistic humility when lining the cages at the veterinary clinic where he held a day job with his own, bylined stories). He later worked for the Los Angeles Times in Sacramento and Los Angeles, and the Orange County Register, before hiring on with his hometown paper, the Daily Camera, where he worked from 1993-2007, and again from 2009-2011.

He also has worked as a barbecue cook for Boulder's late, lamented Wrangler 2, a flower delivery guy for Sturtz& Copeland, a tech for three different vet clinics in California, a lecturer in journalism at CU-Boulder, an administrator and fundraiser — as well as kennel cleaner and adoption counselor — for the Longmont Humane Society, and was Director of Communications for CU Presents, which offers both professional and nonprofessional performing arts programs at CU-Boulder.

Now a freelance writer, he has thousands of bylines to his credit for newspapers, magazines and websites. He has published two previous books, "I See By My Outfit" (Johson Books, 1999), a memoir of his time working as a cowboy, and "The Winter Witch" (Holiday House, 2005), a children's picture book. He currently is working on a nonfiction book related to the story of his grandfather, Alexander Bonnyman Jr., who was posthumously awarded the Medal of Honor after he was killed in the Battle of Tarawa on Nov. 22, 1943. He is also working on a history of the St. Vrain Valley with a focus on water, agriculture and rural life, to be published by Barbed Wire Books in 2016.

He lives in Niwot, Colorado, with his wife, three dogs and two cats, and his stepson is a 2015 graduate of the CU-Boulder College of Engineering. He credits his life-long love of writing (and reading) to his late friend, Ray Bradbury, who taught him that passion is the main ingredient, no matter what you are writing. He is grateful to the Boy Scouts of America and R. Mack Davis for giving him a deep love and respect for the outdoors. He enjoys running, hiking, backpacking, surfing and bicycling — really, just about anything else adventurous that you can do under an open sky.

Although appallingly unhandy himself — the birds refused to move into the birdhouse he made in shop class in seventh grade — he is fiercely loyal to and loves McGuckin Hardware. Where else, after all, can you shop for LED Christmas lights in a "Caribbean" theme of aqua, green and blue (in July), a perfect Swiss humidifier or a replacement Fisher Space Pen or Leatherman tool — indispensable items he has a tendency to lose — while enjoying a bag of Hot Tamales and petting every dog that happens by?

Notes

INTRODUCTION

1 National Hurricane Center, "Saffir Simpson Wind Scale."

2 National Oceanic and Atmospheric Administration, "An Historical Climatology of Damaging Downslope Winds at Boulder, Colorado." Boulder: NOAA, November 1974.

3 Daily Camera, "Eight days, 1,000-year rain, 100-year flood," Sept. 21, 2013

CHAPTER ONE

4 Anna Lee Waldo, "Prairie: The Legend of Charles Burton Irwin and the Y6 Ranch" (New York, 1986), 213-269

5 Department of Historic Resources, state of Virginia, "Jost Hite and Winchester."

CHAPTER TWO

6 Gannett, Henry. "The Origin of Certain Place Names in the United States." Government Printing Office, Washington, D.C., 1905.

7 Harvey, Robert. "Amache: The Story of Japanese Internment in Colorado During World War II." Dallas, Taylor Trade Publishing, 2003.

8 Scarnes, John. "Scarnes' New Complete Guide to Gambling." New York, Fireside, 1986.

CHAPTER THREE

9 Riether, Pat. "Rowdy Earned His Building Tour: Leffingwell's Horse Knew His Way All Around Downtown." Local Color, April 2007. 3-4.

CHAPTER FOUR

10 2014 Colorado Football Information Guide & Record Book. University of Colorado Boulder Athletic Department.

11 "Sunshine to Acquire Gordon in Stock Deal." The Billboard, Sept. 1, 1956.

12 Voynick, Stephen M. "Climax: The History of Colorado's Climax Molybdenum Mine." Mountain Press, 1996. 124-125.

13 Voynick, 125

14 Voynick, 125

15 Voynick, 245

16 Voynick, 244

17 Voynick, 246

CHAPTER FIVE

18 Boulder History Museum. "Timeline: Chief Niwot & Native Americans in Boulder." boulderhistory.org.

19 Lambrecht, Mona and the Boulder History Museum. "Images of America: Boulder 1859-1919." Boulder, Arcadia Publishing, 2008. 9.

20 Ibid, 9

21 Schoolland, J.B. "Boulder in Perspective: From Search for Gold to The Gold of Research." Boulder: Johnson Publishing, 1980. 154.

22 Schoolland, 153

23 Smith, Phyllis. "A Look at Boulder: From Settlement to City." Boulder: Pruett Publishing, 1981. 42.

24 Schoolland, 154.

25 Lambrecht et al. 20.

26 Schoolland. 171.

27 Barker, Jane. "Over the Shoulder" (column). Boulder: Daily Camera, Feb. 6, 1972.

28 Crossen, Forrest. "John W. Valentine recalls his early days in Boulder." Boulder: Daily Camera, Feb. 21, 1955.

29 "Valentine's Beginning 64th Year in Hardware Business on Same Site." Boulder: Daily Camera, Feb. 29, 1968.

30 Daily Camera, Feb. 29, 1968.

31 "John W. Valentine, Leading Boulder Citizen, Dies." Boulder: Daily Camera, Sept. 4, 1956.

32 Meier, Thomas J. "Ed Tangen, The Pictureman: A Photographic History of the Boulder Region, Early Twentieth Century." Boulder: Boulder Creek Press, 1994. 188.

33 Smith, 109.

34 "Widely Known Local Character Dies Sunday." Boulder: Daily Camera,

Aug. 7, 1939.

35 Meier, 188.

36 Boulder: Daily Camera, March 1, 1931.

37 Daily Camera, Feb. 29, 1968.

38 Smith, 207.

39 Riether, 3.

40 "The Second Sale: The Change Is Traded for One or More Screwdrivers." Hardware World, April 5, 1958.

41 "Beech Aircraft Corporation History." Funding Universe, fundinguniverse.com.

42 Smith. 189.

CHAPTER SIX

43 Pettem, Sylvia. "Boulder: A Sense of Time and Place." Longmont: The Book Lode, 2000. 168.

44 Pettem, 167.

45 "Thunderbird Square's Grand Opening Planned." Boulder: Daily Camera, Dec. 12, 1965.

46 Smith, 207.

47 The Encyclopedia of Arkansas History & Culture. "Herbert R. (H.R.) Gibson (1901-1986)." encyclopediaofarkansas.net.

CHAPTER SEVEN

48 Smith, 201.

49 Smith, 201.

50 Smith, 213.

51 Rubino, Joe. "Friends, customers remember Boulder's 'best hardware salesman'." Boulder: Daily Camera, Sept. 6, 2014.

CHAPTER EIGHT

52 Provey, Joseph R. "Build this easy-to-use spinning wheel." Popular Mechanics, September 1979. 105.

53 Pettem, Sylvia. "Harlow Platts inducted into business hall of fame." Boulder: Daily Camera, May 2, 2008.

CHAPTER NINE

54 "Experience Walmart's history." Corporate.walmart.com.

55 "History of Target Through the Years." Corporate.target.com.

56 "A Timeline of the Kmart Corporation." The New York Times, Jan. 22, 2002.

57 Buchanan, Leigh. "The One-Stop Shop for Builders, Inventors and Magicians." Inc., April 6, 2015.

CHAPTER TEN

58 Smith, 231.

59 kineticists.org

60 "True Value Story — True Value Company." truevaluecompany.com

61 Harrington, Maureen. "McGuckin means hardware." Denver: The Denver Post, May 10, 1986.

62 Powers, Monica. "Soviet team finds hardware heaven." Boulder: Daily Camera, May 26, 1989.

CHAPTER ELEVEN

63 Waggoner, Shawn. "Keeping Boulder in good repair." Boulder: Daily Camera, April 23, 1991.

64 Gits, Vicky. "McGuckin planning facelift this summer." Boulder: Daily Camera, May 25, 1993.

65 Ibid

66 Abbott, Karen. "Insider's Guide: Metro Denver hardware stores." Denver: The Denver Post, July 30, 1995.

67 Bradbury, Ray. "Dandelion Wine." New York: Doubleday, 1957.

68 corporate.homedepot.com

69 "Eagle Hardware & Garden, Inc. History." Funding Universe, fundinguniverse.com.

70 Avery, Greg. "Home Depot heads to Boulder." Boulder: Daily Camera, Aug. 6, 2004.

71 "No hardship for hardware." Boulder: Daily Camera, Dec. 17, 1996.

72 Reiner, Eric L. "Boulder family hardware outlet nails competition." Denver: The Denver Post, Aug. 11, 1997.

CHAPTER TWELVE

73 Sheeler, Jim. "Refrigerator magnet pioneer still blooms." Boulder: Boulder Planet, Dec. 2, 1998.

74 Wilke, Steve. "Nuts, Bolts, and Vows." Boulder: Boulder Magazine, getboulder.com, July 2013.

75 Reiner, "Boulder family hardware outlet nails the competition."

76 Avery, Greg. "Home Depot heads to Boulder." Boulder: Daily Camera, Aug. 6, 2004.

77 "Uniquely Independent: Lakewood's Front Range Bank identifies with the mom-and-pop businesses it serves." Denver: Denver Business Journal, May 10, 2002.

CHAPTER THIRTEEN

78 "The Gamow Bag." climbing-high.com

79 "The One-Stop Shop for Builders, Inventors and Magicians." Inc., April 6, 2015.

80 "Maker Friendly Hardware Stores." Makezine.com, April 12, 2014.

CHAPTER FOURTEEN

81 O'Connor, Clare. "Report: Walmart Workers Cost Taxpayers $6.2 Billion in Assistance." Forbes, April 15, 2014.

82 "Just How Wealthy is the Walmart Walton Family?" politifact.com, Dec. 8, 2013.

83 Keillor, Garrison. "Lake Wobegon Days." New York: Penguin, 1986. 118.

84 Hope, Paul. "American Hardware Stores: Nuts and Bolts and Baby Scales." This Old House, June 12, 2014.

85 Decker, Ethan. "Beating Back the Big Boxes." Shopper Culture, shopperculture.com, Oct. 5, 2011.

86 Tayer, John, letter to Daily Camera Pacesetter Awards Committee, Feb. 7, 2015.

87 Leach, Robert. "Political Ideology in Britain." New York: Palgrave Macmillan, 2009. 65.

88 "Offshore Shell Games 2014: The Use of Offshore Tax Havens by Fortune 500 Companies." U.S. Public Interest Research Group Education Fund and Citizens for Tax Justice." June 5, 2014.

89 Wallace, Alica. "Walmart's controversial Boulder grocery store opens, met by 'unwelcome party.'" Boulder: Daily Camera, Oct. 2, 2013.

90 Johnson, J.J., letter to Daily Camera Pacesetter Awards Committee, Feb. 17, 2015.

In Memoriam

The Hight and McGuckin Hardware families fondly remember friends and colleagues who over the years contributed to the McGuckin Way.

Bob Reeves	Meera Narahari
Ed Regel, Sr.	Polly Corwin
Jack Hight	Slick Spaur
Harry T. "Ran" Ransom	Tom Ryken
Pat Hayes	Carmen Desantis
Roger Wood	Stan Anderson
Bill Ekrem	Michelle Eden
Bob Shadel	Cheryl Wynn
Doug Mulder	Charlie Corcoran
Carl Williams	Dave Demarest
Dick Pay	Brenda "Williams" Harrison
Dick Wiggins	Ed Wilkin
Evelyn Carelli	Vince Lockhart
Holly Matthews	Steve Cunningham
Irving Sandvold	Wayne Stockebrand
Jack Leffingwell	Glenn Thomas
Jack Warren	Shawn Melvin
Jim Smittkamp	Don Finch
Keith Krause	Shane Abila
Larry Pardi	Paul Lemmon
Lou Cline	Ken Criswell
Mary Brickner	Tony Bleuze